LAB MANUAL

Customized excerpts from

Windows Server® 2008 Applications Infrastructure Configuration Microsoft Certified Technology Specialist Exam 70-643 Lab Manual

Craig T. Zacker

and

Microsoft® Exchange Server® 2007 Configuration Microsoft Certified Technology Specialist Exam 70-236 Lab Manual

Jason W. Eckert, triOS College

Customized by:
Amado K. Figueroa

The content of this lab manual contains customized excerpts from:

Microsoft® Official Academic Course
Windows Server® 2008 Applications Infrastructure Configuration
Microsoft Certified Technology Specialist Exam 70-643 Lab Manual

And

Microsoft® Official Academic Course
Microsoft® Exchange Server® 2007 Configuration
Microsoft Certified Technology Specialist Exam 70-236 Lab Manual

Since this custom lab manual is based on customized excerpts of the full Microsoft® Official Academic Course lab manuals for 70-643 and 70-236, it is not intended to cover the entire objective domain for these two Microsoft® certification exams. In that way, this custom lab manual is not meant to be a preparatory lab manual for the Microsoft® 70-643 or the Microsoft® 70-236 certification exams.

CUSTOM CONTENTS

Part 2: Customized Excerpts from Microsoft Exchange Server® 2007 Configuration Microsoft Certified Technology Specialist Exam 70-236 Labs

PART 1

Customized Excerpts from

Microsoft® Official Academic Course

Windows Server® 2008 Applications Infrastructure Configuration

Microsoft Certified Technology Specialist Exam 70-643 Lab Manual

LAB 1-1   70-643
PREPARING A VIRTUAL SERVER IMAGE

This lab contains the following exercises:
Exercise 1-1-1 Performing Initial Virtual Server Image
Exercise 1-1-2 Working with Disks

Estimated lab time: 60 minutes

Exercise 1-1-1	Performing Initial Virtual Server Image
Overview	You are creating a new computer virtual appliance with Windows Server 2008 using VMware Player. Your first task is to create a new Virtual Machine and install Windows Server 2008 Standard 32bit with appropriate settings for the test lab network.
Completion time	30 minutes

NOTE: You only have 30 days before activation is required. On day 29 perform the following steps:
- **Click on Start > Accessories, Right mouse click on Command Prompt > select Run as administrator.**
- **Type slmgr –rearm**
- **Wait for the popup screen indicating the process was successful.**
- **Reboot your computer.**

1. Start VMWare Player and create a new Virtual Machine. Make sure that you have your Windows Server 2008 32 bit installation disk in the DVD player.

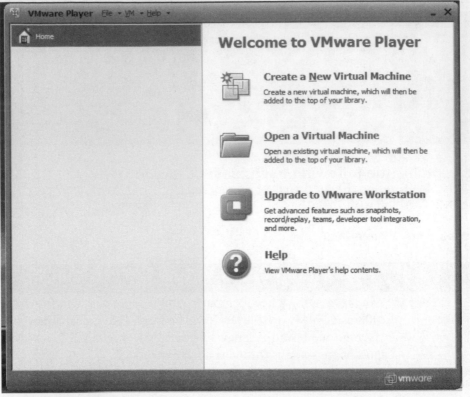

| *Note | Depending on the version of VMWare Player you are using some screens will be slightly different. |

2. Select the installation disk and click next.

3. Skip the Product key and use "Student ##" where ## is the number provided by your instructor as the full name, and P@ssw0rd as password. Select Windows Server 2008 Enterprise.

New Virtual Machine Wizard

Easy Install Information
This is used to install Windows Server 2008.

Windows product <u>k</u>ey

[-   -   -   ]

<u>V</u>ersion of Windows to install

[Windows Server 2008 Enterprise   ▼]

Personalize Windows

<u>F</u>ull name: [Student99]

<u>P</u>assword: [••••••••]   (optional)

<u>C</u>onfirm: [••••••••]

☐ Log on <u>a</u>utomatically (requires a password)

[Help]   [< <u>B</u>ack] [<u>N</u>ext >]   [Cancel]

4. You would like to continue. Click Yes.

VMware Player

? You did not enter a Windows product key. Easy Install may require you to enter it at a later time. Would you like to continue anyway?

[<u>Y</u>es]   [<u>N</u>o]

5. Name your server NT2670-Srv## where ## is the number assigned by your instructor. And store the new Appliance in a newly created NT2670 Server folder in your Virtual machine folder on your removable USB hard disk.

New Virtual Machine Wizard	☒

Name the Virtual Machine
What name would you like to use for this virtual machine?

Virtual machine name:

NT2670-Srv99

Location:

E:\My Virtual Machines\NT2670-Srv99	Browse...

< Back	Next >	Cancel

*Note	Online students can use Student01 as the name of their student account.

*Note	Depending on the version of VMWare Player you are using you may need to choose Windows Server 2008 Standard as the Operating System to install during this step. Please ensure Windows Server 2008 Standard is the version chosen.

6. Click next and choose the default disk size of 40GB, and click next.

New Virtual Machine Wizard   ✕

Specify Disk Capacity
How large do you want this disk to be?

The virtual machine's hard disk is stored as one or more files on the host computer's physical disk. These file(s) start small and become larger as you add applications, files, and data to your virtual machine.

Maximum disk size (GB):   [40.0]

Recommended size for Windows Server 2008: 40 GB

⦿ Store virtual disk as a single file

◯ Split virtual disk into 2 GB files

Splitting the disk makes it easier to move the virtual machine to another computer.

| Help | | < Back | Next > | Cancel |

7. Remember to customize Hardware and select Advance and "legacy systems" for the CD/DVD drive.

New Virtual Machine Wizard   ✕

Ready to Create Virtual Machine
Click Finish to create the virtual machine and start installing Windows Server 2008 and then VMware Tools.

The virtual machine will be created with the following settings:

Name: NT2670-Srv99
Location: E:\My Virtual Machines\NT2670-Srv99
Version: Workstation 6.5-7.0
Operating System: Windows Server 2008

Hard Disk: 40 GB, Split
Memory: 1024 MB
Network Adapter: Host-only
Other Devices: CD/DVD, Floppy, USB Controller, Sound Card

| Customize Hardware... |

☑ Power on this virtual machine after creation

| | < Back | Finish | Cancel |

8. Click finish and install Windows Server 2008 Standard (32bit). Remember uncheck the automatic activation and do not enter a key.

Exercise 1-1-2	Working with Disks
Overview	You will need the new computer to have two installed disk drives. In this exercise, you will create a second Virtual Hard drive. You will then initialize the second disk and create data partitions on the computer.
Completion time	30 minutes

1. Create an additional virtual hard disk drive.
    Open VMWare Player, select your Virtual Machine and Click Edit Virtual
    Machine Settings.

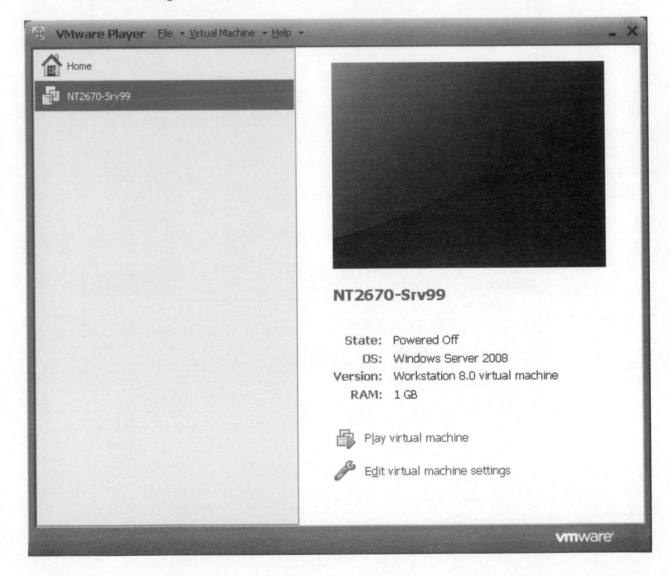

2. Click Add and make sure that Hard Disk is highlighted. Chose next.

3. Choose "Create a new Virtual Hard Disk" and click next.

4. Leave the default "SCSI" and click next.

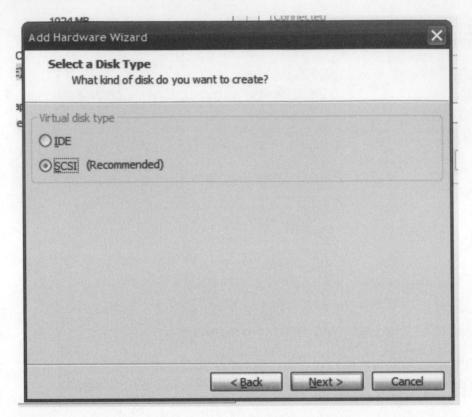

5. Allocate 16 GB, leave the defaults and click next.

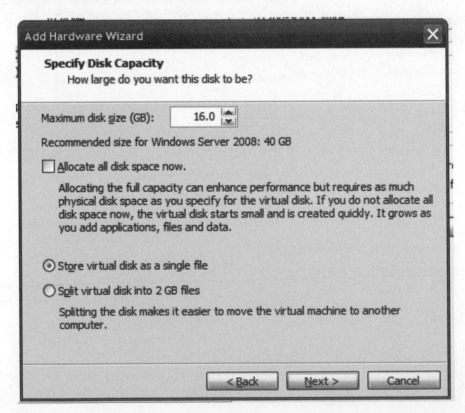

6. Leave the default and click “Finish.”

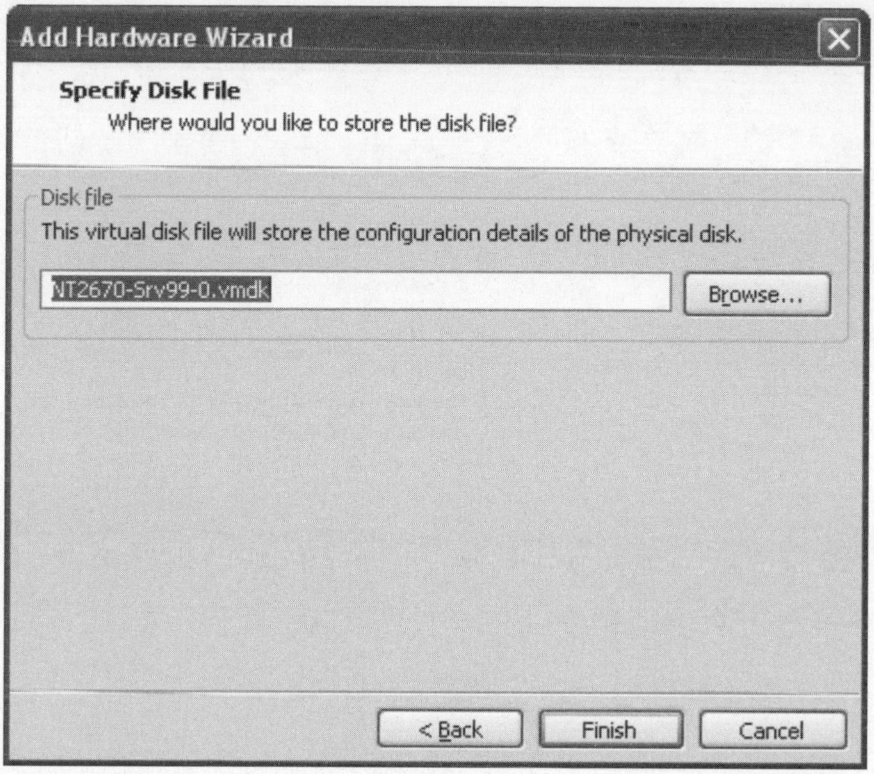

7. You will now see your new Virtual Hard Disk in the Settings.

In order to create free space on your root partition *(40GB)* expand your Virtual HD0 in the Settings menu of VMware Player. Highlight the Hard Disk, select utilities and click Expand.

8. Change the Maximum Disk Size to 80 GB and click Expand.

9. Close the Virtual Machine Settings.

10. While still in the "Settings" Window, click on Network adapter, and Set it to "Host Only."

11. Close the Virtual Machine Settings.
12. After you have finished the installation of your Windows 2008 server and the above exercise, create a second folder in the NT2670 Server folder on your USB removable Hard Drive and copy the contents of your first server folder to this new folder, giving you a second virtual appliance and a baseline backup. This will be the image you use for the NT2670Srv##B required for completion of future labs.

LAB 1-2 70-643
PREPARING AN APPLICATION SERVER

This lab contains the following exercises:

Exercise 1-2-1 Performing Initial Configuration Tasks
Exercise 1-2-2 Working with Disks
Exercise 1-2-3 Using Server Manager
Exercise 1-2-4 Adding the File Services Role
Lab Review: Questions
Lab Challenge: Using Diskpart.exe

Estimated lab time: 70 minutes

BEFORE YOU BEGIN

The classroom network consists of Windows Server 2008 student servers and the ServerDC connected to a local area network. ServerDC, the domain controller for the contoso##.com domain, is running Windows Server 2008. Throughout the labs in this manual, you will install, configure, maintain, and troubleshoot application roles, features, and services on the same student server.

Before you start this lab, see your instructor for the information needed to complete the following table:

Student computer name (NT2670Srv##A)	
Student account name (Student##)	

Working with Lab Worksheets

Each lab in this manual requires that you answer questions, save images of your screen, or perform other activities that you document in a worksheet named for the lab, such as *lab1_2_worksheet*. Your instructor will provide you with the worksheet files that you must complete for each lab. As you perform the exercises in each lab, open the appropriate worksheet file using WordPad, fill in the required information, and save the file to your computer's Student##\Documents folder. Print and turn in a copy of the file for your instructor.

The procedure for opening and saving a worksheet file is as follows:

1.   Open the worksheet document in WordPad.

2.   Complete all of the exercises in the worksheet.

3.   In WordPad, choose Save As from the File menu. The Save As dialog box appears.

4.   In the File Name text box, key **lab##_worksheet_*yourname*** (where lab## contains the number of the lab you're completing, and *yourname* is your last name), and click Save.

5.   Print a copy for your instructor.

SCENARIO

You are a new administrator for Contoso##, Ltd., working on a test deployment of the application server technologies included with Windows Server 2008. In this lab, you prepare a new computer for deployment as a file server.

After completing this lab, you will be able to:

- Perform initial configuration tasks
- Prepare hard disk drives for deployment
- Use the Server Manager console
- Install the File Services role

Exercise 1-2-1	Performing Initial Configuration Tasks
Overview	You are setting up a new computer that was delivered with Windows Server 2008 already installed in its default configuration. Your first task is to configure the computer with appropriate settings for the test lab network.
Completion time	10 minutes

> **NOTE**
>
> *Upon logon you will be prompted to set the password for the Administrator account set it to P@ssw0rd.*

1. Turn on your computer. When the logon screen appears, log on using the local Administrator account and the password *P@ssw0rd*. The Initial Configuration Tasks window appears, as shown in Figure 1-2-1.

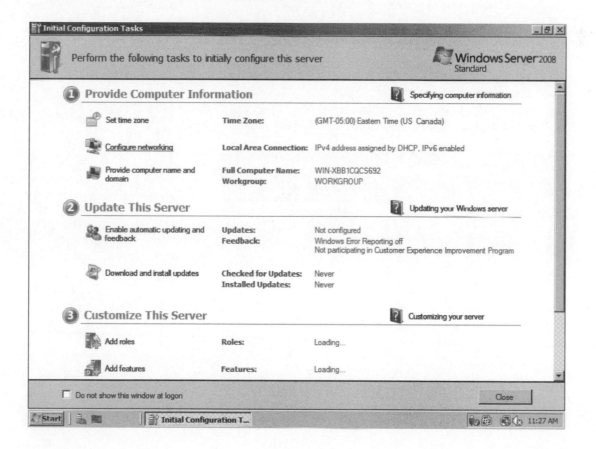

Figure 1-2-1
Initial Configuration Tasks window

2. Click Set Time Zone. The Date And Time dialog box appears.

3. Make sure that the date, time, and time zone shown in the dialog box are correct. If they are not, click Change Date And Time or Change Time Zone and correct them. Then, click OK.

4. Click **Configure Networking**. The Network Connections window appears.

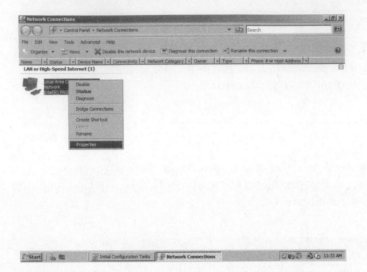

5. Right-click the **Local Area Connection** icon and, from the context menu, select **Properties**.

6. The Local Area Connection Properties sheet appears.

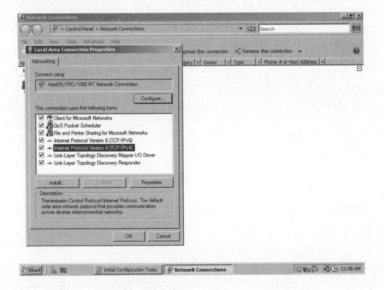

7. Clear the Internet Protocol Version 6 (TCP/IPv6) checkbox.

8. Select **Internet Protocol Version 4 (TCP/IPv4)** and click **Properties**. The Internet Protocol Version 4 (TCP/IPv4) Properties sheet appears.

9. Configure the TCP/IP parameters using the following values:
   - IP Address: 172.16.##.1 (Where ## is the number assigned by your instructor)
   - Subnet Mask: 255.255.255.0
   - Preferred DNS Server: 127.0.0.1

* The IP addresses supplied in this setup document and in the lab manual are suggestions. You can use any IP addresses for the computers in your classroom, as long as all of the systems are located on the same subnet. If the classroom network is connected to a school network or the Internet, you can specify the address of the router providing the network connection in the Default Gateway field. Otherwise, leave it blank.

10. Click **OK** twice to close the two Properties sheets. Close the Network Connections window.

11. Click Provide Computer Name And Domain. The System Properties dialog box appears with the Computer Name tab selected.

12. Click Change. The Computer Name/Domain Changes dialog box appears.

13. In the Computer Name text box, key **NT2670Srv##A** where ##, supplied by your instructor, identifies your computer.

14. Another message box appears, informing you again that you must restart the computer.

15. Click **Restart Now**. The computer restarts.

Your server computer must be an Active Directory domain controller. After the computer restarts, you can install the Active Directory Domain Services role and the Active Directory Domain Services Installation Wizard.

Question 1	*Which computer is hosting the Administrator account that you specified in this authentication?*

INSTALL ACTIVE DIRECTORY
To install Active Directory on NT2670Srv##A, use the following procedure.

INSTALL ACTIVE DIRECTORY

1. Log on with the local Administrator account, using the password **P@ssw0rd**.

2. When the Initial Configuration Tasks window appears, click **Add Roles**. The Add Roles Wizard appears.

3.   Using the Add Roles Wizard, install the Active Directory Domain Services role.

4.   When the role installation is complete, click the **Close this wizard and launch the Active Directory Domain Services Installation Wizard (dcpromo.exe)** link. The *Welcome to the Active Directory Installation Wizard* page appears.

5.   Click **Next** to proceed with the Active Directory installation.

6.   On the *Operating System Compatibility* page, click **Next**.

7.   On the *Choose a Deployment Configuration* page, select **Create a new domain in a new forest** and click **Next**.

8.   On the *Name the Forest Root Domain* page, key **contoso##.com** and click **Next**.

9.   On the *Set the Forest Functional Level* page, click **Next** to accept the default setting.

10. On the *Set Domain Functional Level* page, click **Next** to accept the default setting.

11. On the *Additional Domain Controller Options* page, verify that the **DNS server** checkbox is selected and click **Next**.

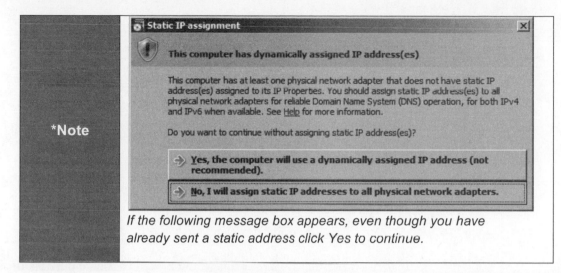

If the following message box appears, even though you have already sent a static address click Yes to continue.

12. A message box appears, warning you that the system cannot locate an existing DNS infrastructure.

13. Because you will be creating a new DNS infrastructure, you can ignore this warning and click **Yes**.

14. On the *Location for Database, Log Files, and SYSVOL* page, click **Next** to accept the default settings.

15. On the *Directory Services Restore Mode Administrator Password* page, key **P@ssw0rd** in the Password and Confirm Password text boxes and click **Next**.

16. On the *Summary* page, click **Next**.

17. When the installation process is complete, restart the server.

18. After the server restarts, it functions as the domain controller for the contoso##.com domain.

INSTALLING THE DHCP SERVER ROLE
To install the DHCP server on NT2670Srv##A, use the following procedure.

INSTALL THE DHCP SERVER ROLE

1. Log on with the domain Administrator account using the password **P@ssw0rd**.

2. When the Initial Configuration Tasks window appears, click **Add Roles**. The Add Roles Wizard appears.

3. Using the Add Roles Wizard, install the DHCP Server role.

4. On the *Select Network Connection Bindings* page, click **Next** to accept the default settings.

5. On the *Specify IPv4 DNS Server Settings* page, click **Next** to accept the default settings.

6. On the *Specify IPv4 WINS Server Settings* page, click **Next** to accept the default settings.

7. On the *Add or Edit DHCP Scopes* page, click **Add**.

8. In the Add Scope dialog box, create a scope using the following values:
   • Scope Name: Classroom ##
   • Starting IP Address: 172.16.##.101
   • Ending IP Address: 172.16.##.150
   • Subnet Mask: 255.255.255.0
   • Subnet Type: Wired

9. Select the **Activate this scope** checkbox and click **OK**. Then click **Next**.

10. On the Configure DHCPv6 Stateless Mode pane, Choose "Disable DHCPv6 Stateless Mode on this server" and click **Next**.

11. On the *Authorize DHCP Server* page, click **Next** to accept the default settings.

12. On the *Confirm Installation Selections* page, click **Install**.

13. **CLOSE** the Initial Configuration Tasks window when the installation is complete.

After the DHCP role is installed, all student servers will obtain their IP addresses and other TCP/IP configuration settings via DHCP.

Creating User Accounts

Each student must have a domain user account called Student##, where ## is the same number as the computer the student is using. To create the student accounts, use the following procedure. **(Note that this account might have been created during the initial Server 2008 installation, but the group memberships will still need to be configured.)**

CREATE USER ACCOUNTS

1. Click **Start**, and then select **Administrative Tools** > **Active Directory Users and Computers**. The Active Directory Users and Computers console appears.
2. Expand the contoso##.com domain. If the **Student##** account already exists skip to step 8.
3. Right-click the **Users** container and select **New** > **User**. The New Object-User wizard appears.
4. Key **Student##** in the First Name and User Logon Name text boxes, where ## is the number assigned by your instructor. Then click **Next**.
5. In the Password and Confirm Password text boxes, key **P@ssw0rd**.
6. Clear the **User Must Change Password At Next Logon** checkbox and select the **Password Never Expires** checkbox. Then click **Next**.

7. Click OK.
8. Right-click the Users container and select New > Group. The New Object-Group wizard appears.

9. In the Group Name text box, key Students. Accept the defaults and click OK.
10. In the Users container, double-click the Students group you just created. The Students Properties sheet appears.
11. Click the **Members** tab.
12. Click **Add**, key the name of the Student## user you created, and click **OK**.
13. Using the same procedure, open the Properties sheet for the Domain Admins group and add the Students group you created as members of that group.
14. **CLOSE** the Active Directory Users and Computers console.

The students will use these Student## accounts to log on to the domain as they complete the exercises in the lab manual. Their membership in the Students group provides domain Administrator privileges, as well as local Administrator privileges on their individual servers.

NOTE

Completing the initial configuration tasks in this exercise leaves the student computer in its baseline state, which is the computer's expected configuration at the beginning of each subsequent lab. If your class uses virtual machines, you might have to repeat the steps of this exercise before you begin each lab.

Exercise 1-2-2	Working with Disks
Overview	The new computer arrived with two installed disk drives, but only the first one is initialized and partitioned. In this exercise, you will initialize the second disk and create data partitions on the computer.
Completion time	20 minutes

1. Click Start, and then click Administrative Tools > Computer Management. A User Account Control dialog box may appear, prompting you for your permission to continue.

2. Click Continue. The Computer Management console appears.

3. In the Computer Management console's scope (left) pane, select Disk Management. The Disk Management snap-in appears in the details (right) pane, as shown in Figure 1-2-2.

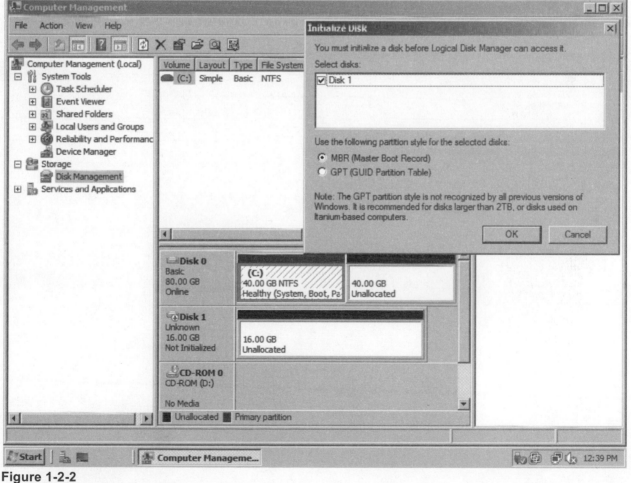

Figure 1-2-2
Disk Management snap-in

4. Immediately after the snap-in appears, an Initialize Disk dialog box appears, prompting you to select a partition style for Disk 1. Leave the default MBR (Master Boot Record) option selected, and click OK.

Question 2	Why is the system prompting you to initialize Disk 1 at this time?
Question 3	What happens to the Disk 1 type and status when the initialization process is complete?
Question 4	Now that Disk 1 has been initialized, why doesn't it appear in the volume list pane at the top of the console?

5. Based on the information displayed in the Disk Management snap-in, fill out the information in Table 1-2-1 on your lab worksheet.

Table 1-2-1

Disk information

	Disk 0	Disk 1
Disk type (basic or dynamic)		
Total disk size		
Number and type of partitions		
Amount of unallocated space		

NOTE

If at least ten gigabytes of unallocated space is not available on your workstation's Disk 0, expand your Virtual HD0 in the Settings menu of VMware player to 80GB before you continue.

Expand Disk Capacity   ☒

Specify the maximum size for the virtual disk:

Maximum disk size (GB):   80 ⏶⏷

ⓘ Expand increases only the size of a virtual disk. Sizes of partitions and file systems are not affected.

| Expand | Cancel | Help |

VMware Player

Expanding virtual disk...

Cancel

6. In the graphical display, right-click the Unallocated area of Disk 0 and, from the context menu, select New Simple Volume. The New Simple Volume Wizard appears.

7. Click Next to bypass the *Welcome* page. The *Specify Volume Size* page appears.

8. In the Simple Volume Size In MB text box, key **5000** and click Next. The *Assign Drive Letter Or Path* page appears.

9. Leave the Assign The Following Drive Letter radio button selected, select drive letter X from the drop-down list, and click Next. The *Format Partition* page appears.

10. Leave the Format This Partition With The Following Settings radio button selected, and configure the next three parameters as follows:

- File System: NTFS

- Allocation Unit Size: Default

- Volume Label: Data1

11. Select the Perform A Quick Format checkbox and click Next. The *Completing The New Simple Volume Wizard* page appears.

12. Click Finish. The new Data1 volume appears in the console.

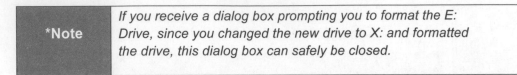

*Note	If you receive a dialog box prompting you to format the E: Drive, since you changed the new drive to X: and formatted the drive, this dialog box can safely be closed.

13. Using the same procedure, create another simple volume using the rest of the unallocated space on Disk 0, assigning it the drive letter Y and the volume name Data2.

14. Right-click the Data2 volume you created. A context menu appears.

Question 5	What volume sizing options are available in the context menu?
Question 6	Why are you unable to extend the Data2 volume to Disk 1?

15. Right-click Disk 0 and, from the context menu, select Convert To Dynamic Disk. The Convert To Dynamic Disk dialog box appears.

16. Click OK. The Disks To Convert dialog box appears.

17. Click Convert. A Disk Management message box appears containing a warning about boot limitations from dynamic disks.

18. Click Yes. Disk 0 changes from a basic to a dynamic disk.

19. Right-click the Data2 volume and, from the context menu, select Extend Volume. The Extend Volume Wizard appears.

20. Click Next to bypass the *Welcome* page. The *Select Disks* page appears.

21. Select Disk 1 in the Available box, and click Add. Disk 1 moves to the Selected box.

22. Using the Select The Amount Of Space In MB spin box, allocate approximately half of the available space on Disk 1 to the Data2 volume.

23. Click Next. The *Completing The Extend Volume Wizard* page appears.

24. Click Finish. A Disk Management message box appears, informing you that the process of extending the volume will cause the selected basic disk to be converted to a dynamic disk.

Question 7	Why is it necessary to convert both of the disks?

25. Click Yes. The Data2 volume is extended to include half of the available space on Disk 1.

26. Repeat the procedure to extend the volume in Disk 0 containing the C: drive to the remaining space on Disk 1.

Question 8	Why are you unable to extend the C: drive to Disk 1?

27. Consult the Disk Management snap-in, and fill out Table 1-2-2 with the amount of unallocated space on the drive in gigabytes and megabytes.

Table 1-2-2
Unallocated space remaining

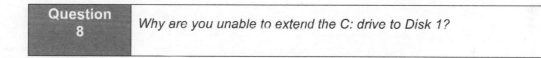

	Disk 0	Disk 1
Unallocated space left (in gigabytes)		
Unallocated space left (in megabytes)		

28. Press Ctrl+Prt Scr to take a screen shot of the Disk Management snap-in showing the volumes you created. Press Ctrl+V to paste the image on the page provided in the lab1_2_worksheet file.

29. Close the Computer Management console, and leave the computer logged on for the next exercise.

Exercise 1-2-3	Using Server Manager
Overview	In the future, you will need to configure your server to perform certain tasks, using tools and services that Windows Server 2008 does not install by default. In this exercise, use the Server Manager console to configure the server and install these tools and services.
Completion time	10 minutes

1.   Click Start, point to Administrative Tools, and click Server Manager. Click Continue in the User Account Control message box. The Server Manager console appears, as shown in Figure 1-2-3.

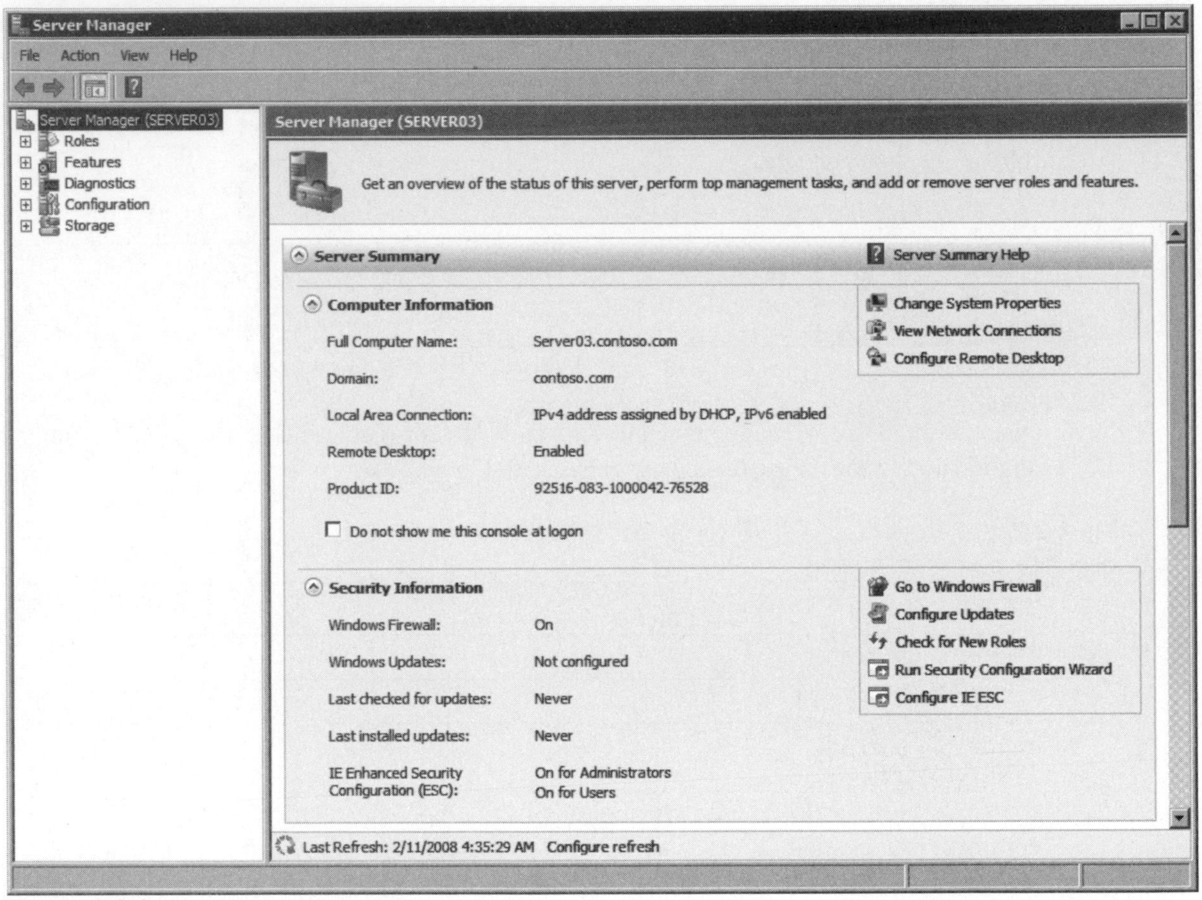

Figure 1-2-3
Server Manager console

Question 9	Which of the previous tasks could be completed using Server Manager instead of other consoles?

2. In the Server Summary section under Security Information, click Configure IE ESC. The Internet Explorer Enhanced Security Configuration dialog box appears.

3. Under Administrators, select the Off option, and click OK.

Question 10	Based on the information in the main Server Manager display, what roles are currently installed on the computer?
Question 11	What features are currently installed on the computer?

4. In the scope pane, select the Features node, and click Add Features. The Add Features Wizard appears, displaying the *Select Features* page.

5. Select the Group Policy Management checkbox.

6. Expand Remote Server Administration Tools and Role Administration Tools. Then, select the Active Directory Domain Services Tools checkbox, and click Next. The *Confirm Installation Selections* page appears.

7. Click Install. The wizard installs the features you selected.

8. Click Close. Restart the computer when prompted.

9. When the computer restarts, log on using your domain Administrator account. The Server Manager console opens, and the Resume Configuration Wizard appears.

Question 12	What was the result of the installation?

10. Press Ctrl+Prt Scr to take a screen shot of the *Installation Results* page in the Resume Configuration Wizard. Press Ctrl+V to paste the image on the page provided in the lab1_2_worksheet file.

11. Click Close.

12. Leave Server Manager open for the next exercise.

Exercise 1-2-4   Adding the File Services Role

Overview	Install the File Services role by using the Server Manager console. This enables you to deploy this computer as a file server and implement the various storage-related technologies supplied with Windows Server 2008.
Completion time	10 minutes

1. In the Server Manager scope pane, select the Roles node, and then click Add Roles. The Add Roles Wizard appears, displaying the *Before You Begin* page.

2. Click Next. The *Select Server Roles* page appears, as shown in Figure 1-2-4.

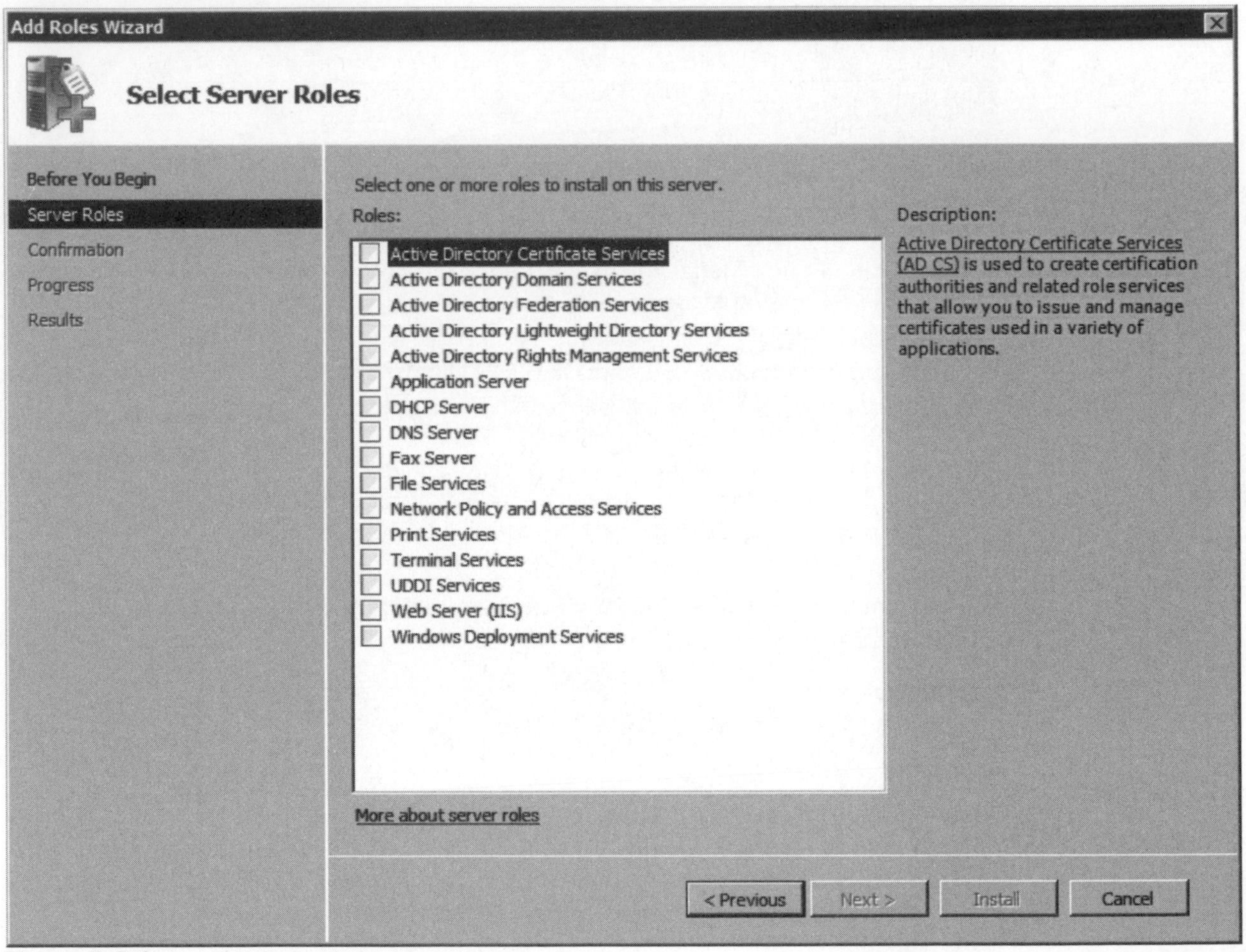

Figure 1-2-4
Select Server Roles page of the Add Roles Wizard

3.   Select the File Services checkbox, and click Next.

Question 13	What happens to the wizard when you select the File Services checkbox?

4.   Click Next to bypass the *Introduction To File Services* page. The *Select Role Services* page appears.

5.   Select the Services For Network File System and Windows Search Service role service checkboxes.

Question 14	What happens to the wizard when you select the Windows Search Services checkbox?
Question 15	What happens to the wizard if you select the Windows Server 2003 File Services checkbox?

6.   Click Next to continue. The *Volumes To Index* page appears.

7.   Select the Local Disk (C:) checkbox, and click Next. The *Confirmation* page appears.

8.   Click Install. The wizard installs the role and the selected role services.

9.   Click Close to close the wizard.

10. Press Ctrl+Prt Scr to take a screen shot of the Roles node in server manager, showing the details for the installed File Services role. Press Ctrl+V to paste the image on the page provided in the lab1_2_worksheet file.

11. Close Server Manager and leave the computer logged on for the next exercise.

LAB REVIEW: QUESTIONS

Completion time	5 minutes

1.   After creating a spanned volume containing space from two disks, as you did in Exercise 1-2-2, what happens to the data stored on the volume if Disk 1 fails?

2.   In Exercise 1-2-2, how many partitions does each disk have after you converted the disks from basic to dynamic? How do you know?

3.   In Exercise 1-2-3, what is the effect of turning off Internet Explorer Enhanced Security Configuration?

LAB CHALLENGE: USING DISKPART.EXE

Completion time	15 minutes

Your supervisor wants to use the Windows Server 2008 Server Core option to deploy servers on the network. This means that most of the graphical system administration tools will not be available on these computers, so you have to brush up your command prompt skills. You must extend the spanned volume you created in Exercise 1.2 (Data2) to use all of the available disk space on Disk 1. However, you cannot use the Disk Management snap-in; you must use only the Diskpart.exe command-prompt utility.

To complete this challenge, write a procedure for completing your task, including all of the needed Diskpart commands. When you have successfully extended the spanned volume, open the Disk Management snap-in, and take a screen shot showing the volumes on the computer. Paste the image on the page provided in the lab1_2_worksheet file.

LAB 1-3
CREATING USERS WITH A BATCH FILE

This lab contains the following exercises:

Exercise 1-3-1 Creating Users Using DSAdd

Estimated lab time: 20 minutes

Exercise 1-3-1	Creating Users Using DSAdd
Overview	You need to add users to Active Directory, while there are a few ways to complete this task, your Senior Administrator would like you to create a batch file in notepad that can be edited in the future. In this lab you will use notepad to create and execute a batch file to automate the task of adding users.
Completion time	20 minutes

1. Click Start > All Programs >Accessories > Notepad. The Notepad window appears.

2. In the Notepad window enter:
    dsadd user "CN=User1,CN=Users,DC=Contoso##,DC=Com" –pwd P@ssw0rd

Question 1	What would be the syntax to add an OU named Marketing?

Question 2	What does the –pwd switch do? How can you make DSadd bring up a prompt asking for the users password?

3. Cut and paste the dsadd command from step two and edit it to add the following users:
    (*Use the first initial – last name naming convention i.e. Mark Jones = MJones)
    a. Mark Jones
    b. John Stafford
    c. Peter King
    d. Bill Elliot
    e. Larry Johnson
    f. Edward Williams
    g. David West

4. Save the Notepad file as Users.Bat

*Note	*User accounts should be consistent. Capital initial from first name and capital character for first letter of last name.*

```
Users - Notepad                                                    _|□|×|
File  Edit  Format  View  Help
dsadd user  "CN=User1,cn=users,dc=contoso99,dc=com"  -pwd P@ssw0rd
dsadd user  "CN=MJones,cn=users,dc=contoso99,dc=com"  -pwd P@ssw0rd
dsadd user  "CN=JStafford,cn=users,dc=contoso99,dc=com"  -pwd P@ssw0rd
dsadd user  "CN=PKing,cn=users,dc=contoso99,dc=com"  -pwd P@ssw0rd
dsadd user  "CN=BElliot,cn=users,dc=contoso99,dc=com"  -pwd P@ssw0rd
dsadd user  "CN=LJohnson,cn=users,dc=contoso99,dc=com"  -pwd P@ssw0rd
dsadd user  "CN=EWilliams,cn=users,dc=contoso99,dc=com"  -pwd P@ssw0rd
dsadd user  "CN=DWest,cn=users,dc=contoso99,dc=com"  -pwd P@ssw0rd
```

5. Double click the Users.bat file to execute it.

6. Open Active Directory Users and Computer and browse to your Users container. Take a screen shot of the Active Directory Users and Computers snap-in that shows the users you created by pressing Alt + Prt Scr, and the paste the resulting image into the Lab1_3_worksheet file in the page provided by pressing Ctrl + V.

7. Open a new Notepad file use your answer to question 1 to create the following OUs:
    a. Marketing
    b. Sales
    c. Finance
    d. Management

8. Save the Notepad file as OU.Bat

```
Users - Notepad
File  Edit  Format  View  Help
dsadd user "CN=User1,cn=users,dc=contoso99,dc=com" -pwd P@ssw0rd
dsadd user "CN=MJones,cn=users,dc=contoso99,dc=com" -pwd P@ssw0rd
dsadd user "CN=JStafford,cn=users,dc=contoso99,dc=com" -pwd P@ssw0rd
dsadd user "CN=PKing,cn=users,dc=contoso99,dc=com" -pwd P@ssw0rd
dsadd user "CN=BElliot,cn=users,dc=contoso99,dc=com" -pwd P@ssw0rd
dsadd user "CN=LJohnson,cn=users,dc=contoso99,dc=com" -pwd P@ssw0rd
dsadd user "CN=EWilliams,cn=users,dc=contoso99,dc=com" -pwd P@ssw0rd
dsadd user "CN=DWest,cn=users,dc=contoso99,dc=com" -pwd P@ssw0rd
```

9. Double click the OU.bat file to execute it.

10. Open Active Directory Users and Computer and browse to your Users container. Take a screen shot of the Active Directory Users and Computers snap-in that shows the organizational units you created by pressing Alt + Prt Scr, and the paste the resulting image into the Lab1_3_worksheet file in the page provided by pressing Ctrl + V.

LAB 2-1 70-643
PREPARING A SECOND APPLICATION SERVER

This lab contains the following exercises:

Exercise 2-1-1 Performing Initial Configuration Tasks
Exercise 2-1-2 Using Server Manager
Exercise 2-1-3 Adding the File Services Role
Exercise 2-1-4 Installing an Additional Domain Controller
Lab Review: Questions

Estimated lab time: 75 minutes

BEFORE YOU BEGIN

The classroom network consists of Windows Server 2008 student server A (NT2670Srv##A) and B (NT2670Srv##B) a connected to via an internal local area network. NT2670Srv##A the domain controller for the contoso##.com domain, is running Windows Server 2008. Throughout the labs in this manual, you will install, configure, maintain, and troubleshoot application roles, features, and services on the NT2670Srv##B.

Before you start this lab, see your instructor for the information needed to complete the following table:

Student computer name (NT2670Srv##B)	
Student account name (Student##)	

Working with Lab Worksheets

Each lab in this manual requires that you answer questions, save images of your screen, or perform other activities that you document in a worksheet named for the lab and task, such as *lab2_1 _worksheet*. Your instructor provided you with lab worksheets. As you perform the tasks and exercises in each lab, open the appropriate worksheet file using WordPad, fill in the required information, and save the file to your computer's Student##\Documents folder. Print a copy for your instructor.

The procedure for opening and saving a worksheet file is as follows:

1. Open worksheet document opens in WordPad.

2. Complete all of the exercises in the worksheet.

3. In WordPad, choose Save As from the File menu. The Save As dialog box appears.

4. In the File Name text box, key **lab##_ worksheet_*yourname*** (where lab##_task## contains the number of the lab and task you're completing, and *yourname* is your last name), and click Save.

5. Print a copy for your instructor.

SCENARIO

You are a new administrator for Contoso##, Ltd., working on a test deployment of the application server technologies included with Windows Server 2008. In this lab, you prepare a new computer for deployment as a file server.

After completing this lab, you will be able to:

- Perform initial configuration tasks
- Prepare hard disk drives for deployment
- Use the Server Manager console
- Install the File Services role

Exercise 2-1-1 Performing Initial Configuration Tasks

Overview	You are setting up a new computer that was delivered with Windows Server 2008 already installed in its default configuration. Your first task is to configure the computer with appropriate settings for the test lab network.
Completion time	10 minutes

> **NOTE**
> *Upon logon on the NT2670Srv##B computer you will be prompted to set the password for the Administrator account set it to P@ssw0rd.*

1. Start your NT2670Srv##A and NT2670Srv##B computers. On the NT2670SRV##B computer when the logon screen appears, log on using the local Administrator account and the password *P@ssw0rd*. The Initial Configuration Tasks window appears, as shown in Figure 2-1-1.

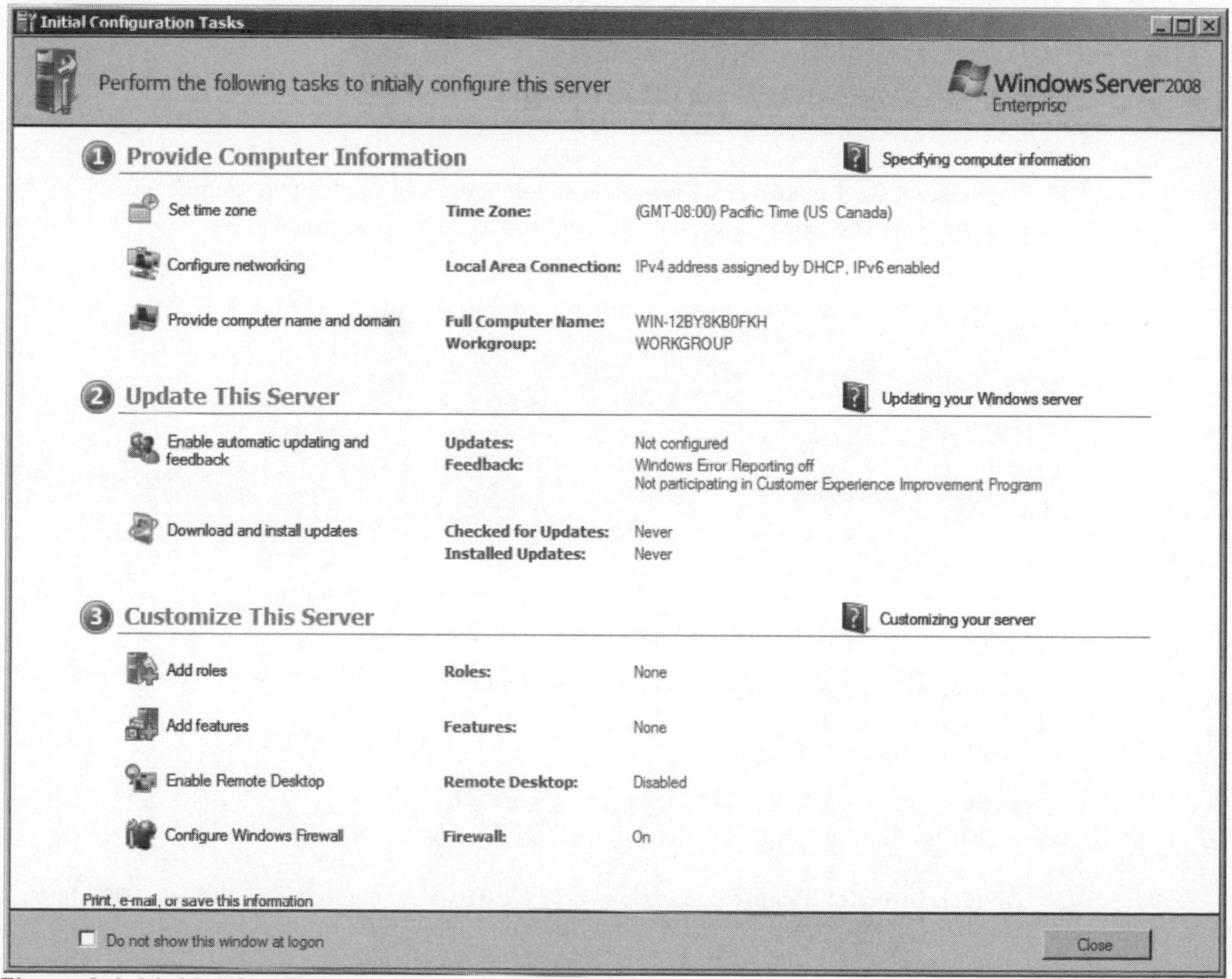

Figure 2-1-1 Initial Configuration Tasks window

2. Click Set Time Zone. The Date And Time dialog box appears.

3. Make sure that the date, time, and time zone shown in the dialog box are correct. If they are not, click Change Date And Time or Change Time Zone and correct them. Then, click OK.

4. Click **Configure Networking**. The Network Connections window appears.

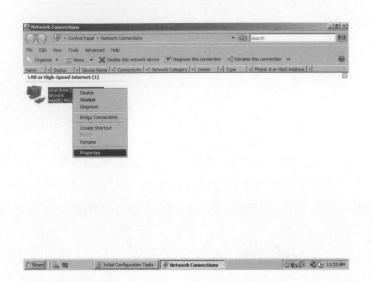

5. Right-click the **Local Area Connection** icon and, from the context menu, select **Properties**. The Local Area Connection Properties sheet appears.

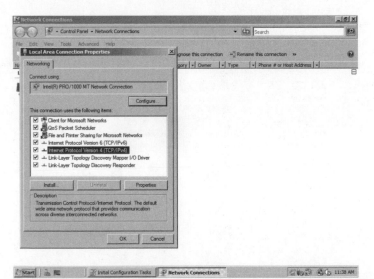

6. Clear the Internet Protocol Version 6 (TCP/IPv6) checkbox.

7. Select **Internet Protocol Version 4 (TCP/IPv4)** and click **Properties**. The Internet Protocol Version 4 (TCP/IPv4) Properties sheet appears.

8. Configure the TCP/IP parameters using the following values:

    • IP Address: 172.16.##.2 (Where ## is the number assigned by your instructor)
    • Subnet Mask: 255.255.255.0
    • Preferred DNS Server: 172.16.##.1

9. Click Provide Computer Name And Domain. The System Properties dialog box appears with the Computer Name tab selected.

10. Click Change. The Computer Name/Domain Changes dialog box appears.

11. In the Computer Name text box, key **NT2670Srv##B**, where ##, supplied by your instructor, identifies your computer.

12. Select the Domain option key **contoso##.com** in the text box, and click OK. A Windows Security dialog box appears.

13. In the User Name test box, key **Administrator**. Key **P@ssw0rd** in the Password text box, and click OK. A message box appears, welcoming you to the contoso.com domain.

Computer Name/Domain Changes

You can change the name and the membership of this computer. Changes might affect access to network resources. More information

Computer name:

```
NT2670Srv99B
```

Full computer name:
NT2670Srv99B

More...

Member of
○ Domain:
```
Contoso10.Com
```
○ Workgroup:
```
WORKGROUP
```

OK   Cancel

Question 1	Which computer is hosting the Administrator account that you specified in this authentication?

14. Click OK. A message box appears, prompting you to restart your computer.

15. Click OK, and then click Close to close the System Properties dialog box. Another message box appears, informing you again that you must restart the computer.

16. Click Restart Now. The computer restarts.

17. Log on to the domain with your *Administrator* account, using the password *P@ssw0rd*.

18. Press Ctrl+Prt Scr to take a screen shot of the Initial Configuration Tasks window, and then press Ctrl+V to paste the image on the page provided in the lab2_1 _worksheet file.

19. Leave the computer logged on for the next exercise.

Completing the initial configuration tasks in this exercise leaves the student computer in its baseline state, which is the computer's expected configuration at the beginning of each subsequent lab. If your class uses virtual machines, you might have to repeat the steps of this exercise before you begin each lab.

Exercise 2-1-2   Using Server Manager

Overview	In the future, you will need to configure your server to perform certain tasks, using tools and services that Windows Server 2008 does not install by default. In this exercise, use the Server Manager console to configure the server and install these tools and services.
Completion time	10 minutes

1. Click Start, point to Administrative Tools, and click Server Manager. The Server Manager console appears, as shown in Figure 2-1-2.

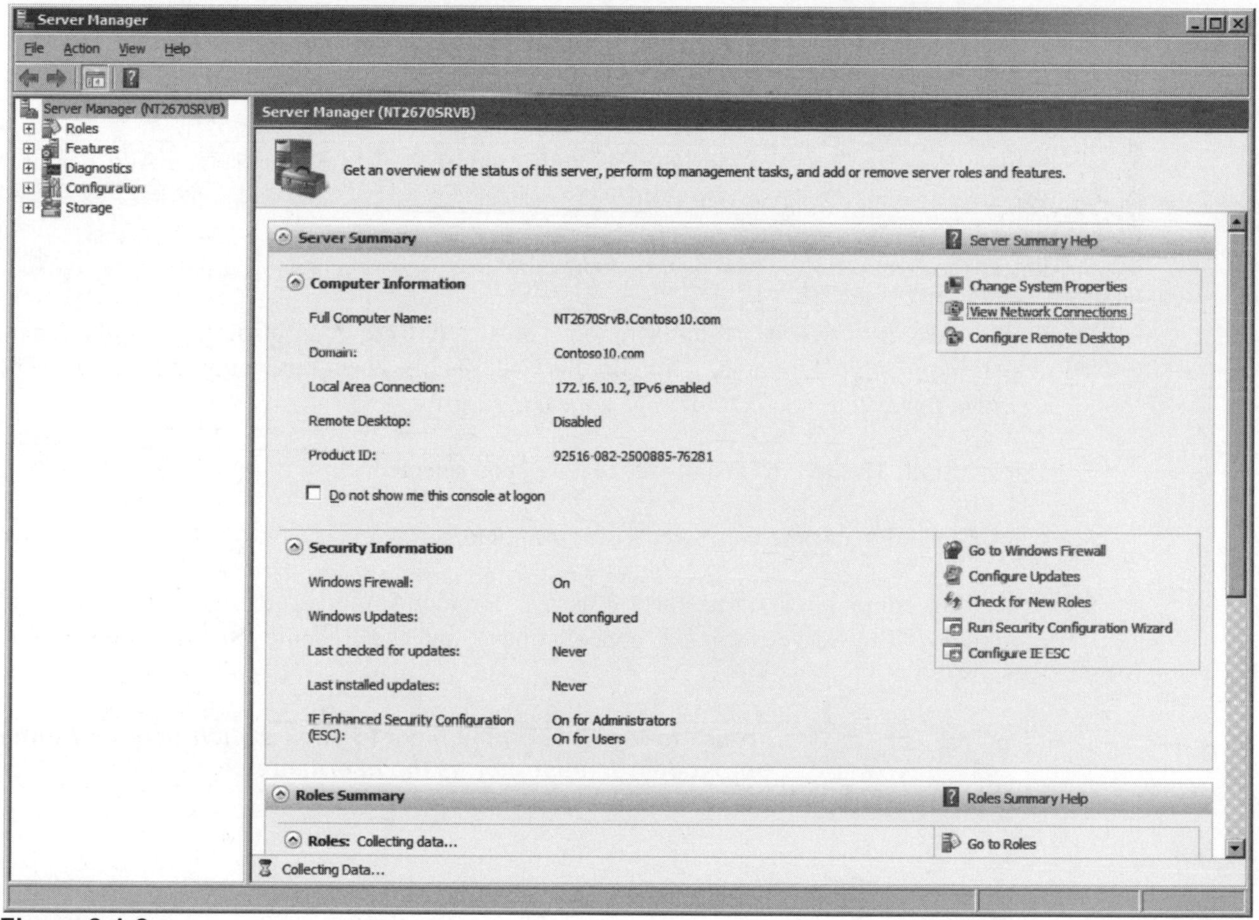

Figure 2-1-2
Server Manager Console

Question 2	Which of the previous tasks could be completed using Server Manager instead of other consoles?

2. In the Server Summary section under Security Information, click Configure IE ESC. The Internet Explorer Enhanced Security Configuration dialog box appears.

3. Under Administrators, select the Off option, and click OK.

Question 3	Based on the information in the main Server Manager display, what roles are currently installed on the computer?
Question 4	What features are currently installed on the computer?

4. In the scope pane, select the Features node, and click Add Features. The Add Features Wizard appears, displaying the *Select Features* page.

5. Select the Group Policy Management checkbox.

6. Expand Remote Server Administration Tools and Role Administration Tools. Then, select the Active Directory Domain Services Tools checkbox, and click Next. The *Confirm Installation Selections* page appears.

7. Click Install. The wizard installs the features you selected.

8. Click Close. Restart the computer when prompted.

9. When the computer restarts, log on as the domain Administrator using the password *P@ssw0rd*. The Server Manager console opens, and the Resume Configuration Wizard appears.

Note	**In order to log in you may have to click switch user and enter Contoso##\Administrator as the username.**

Question 5	What was the result of the installation?

10. Press Ctrl+Prt Scr to take a screen shot of the *Installation Results* page in the Resume Configuration Wizard. Press Ctrl+V to paste the image on the page provided in the lab2_1_ worksheet file.

11. Click Close.

12. Leave Server Manager open for the next exercise.

Exercise 2-1-3	Adding the File Services Role
Overview	Install the File Services role by using the Server Manager console. This enables you to deploy this computer as a file server and implement the various storage-related technologies supplied with Windows Server 2008.
Completion time	10 minutes

1. In the Server Manager scope pane, select the Roles node, and then click Add Roles. The Add Roles Wizard appears, displaying the *Before You Begin* page.

2. Click Next. The *Select Server Roles* page appears, as shown in Figure 2-1-3.

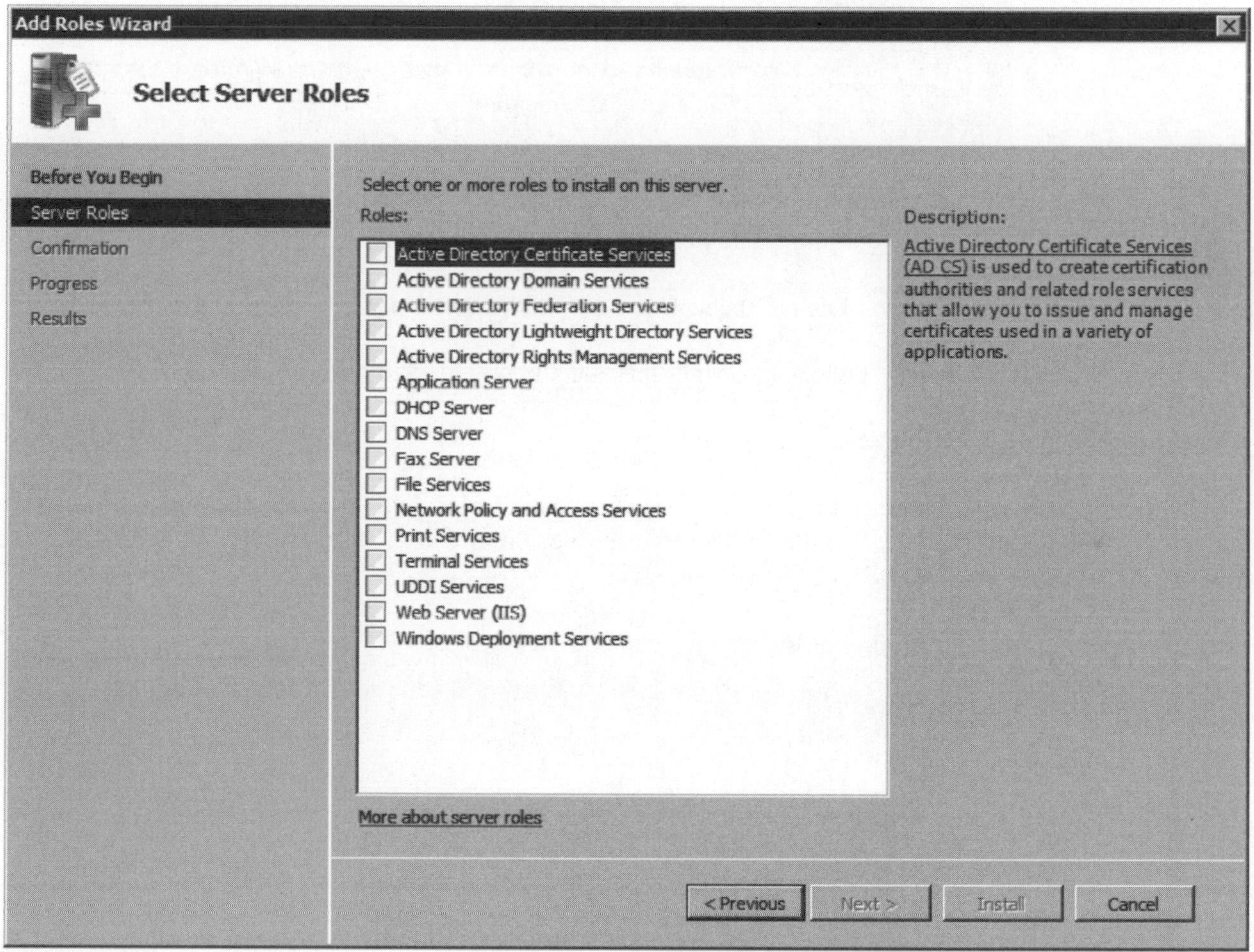

Figure 2-1-3
Select Server Roles page of the Add Roles Wizard

3. Select the File Services checkbox, and click Next.

Question 6	What happens to the wizard when you select the File Services checkbox?

4. Click Next to bypass the *Introduction To File Services* page. The *Select Role Services* page appears.

5. Select the Services For Network File System and Windows Search Service role service checkboxes.

Question 7	What happens to the wizard when you select the Windows Search Services checkbox?
Question 8	What happens to the wizard if you select the Windows Server 2003 File Services checkbox?

6. Click Next to continue. The *Volumes To Index* page appears.

7. Select the Local Disk (C:) checkbox, and click Next. The *Confirmation* page appears.

8. Click Install. The wizard installs the role and the selected role services.

9. Click Close to close the wizard.

10. Press Ctrl+Prt Scr to take a screen shot of the Roles node in server manager, showing the details for the installed File Services role. Press Ctrl+V to paste the image on the page provided in the lab2_1_worksheet file.

11. Leave the computer logged on for the next exercise.

Exercise 2-1-4   Installing an Additional Domain Controller

Overview	In the following exercise, you install Active Directory on NT2670Srv##B as the second domain controller in an existing domain in an existing forest. Before running the Active Directory installation wizard, you must first ensure NT2670##B is configured to use NT2670##A for DNS name resolution (as configured in Exercise 1-2-1). To complete this lab exercise, NT2670##A and NT2670##B must be started and have network access.
Completion time	40 minutes

1. On NT2670Srv##B click Start, and then click Run. In the Run dialog box, type **dcpromo** and press Enter.

2. When the Active Directory Installation Wizard appears, click Next.

3. At the Operating System Compatibility page, click Next.

4. At the Domain Controller Type page ensure that **Existing Forest > Add a domain controller to an existing domain** is selected and click Next.

5. At the Network Credentials page, leave the **My current logged on credentials** option selected and enter **contoso##.com** as the domain.

6. At the Select a domain page, ensure that contoso##.com is listed as the DNS name of the existing domain in the forest. Click Next when finished.

7. Click Next to accept the Default-First-Site-Name site.

8. At the Additional domain controllers options window click Next to accept the default options. One or more Active Directory Domain Services Installation Wizard warning windows are displayed sequentially.

9. Read each warning and click Yes to continue.

10. At the Database and Log Folders page, review the default location for the AD database and database logs and click Next.

11. At the Directory Services Restore Mode Administrator Password page, enter **P@ssw0rd** in both password dialog boxes and click Next.

12. At the Summary page, review your installation choices and click Next.

13. After the installation has completed, click the Finish button. Click **Restart Now** when prompted to restart your domain controller.

LAB REVIEW: QUESTIONS

Completion time	5 minutes

1. In Exercise 2-1-1, what credentials were required to join the contoso.com domain?

2. In Exercise 2-1-2, what is the effect of turning off Internet Explorer Enhanced Security Configuration?

LAB 2-2 70-643 DEPLOYING A WEB SERVER

This lab contains the following exercises:

Exercise 2-2-1 Installing the Web Server (IIS) Role
Exercise 2-2-2 Configuring Web Server Properties
Exercise 2-2-3 Preparing Web Site Content
Exercise 2-2-4 Creating Web Sites
Exercise 2-2-5 Creating Virtual Directories
Lab Review: Questions
Lab Challenge: Creating Port Number Bindings

Estimated lab time: 85 minutes

BEFORE YOU BEGIN

The classroom network consists of Windows Server 2008 student server A and B a connected to via an internal local area network. NT2670Srv##A the domain controller for the contoso.com domain, is running Windows Server 2008. Throughout the labs in this manual, you will install, configure, maintain, and troubleshoot application roles, features, and services on the NT2670Srv##A.

To accommodate various types of classroom arrangements, each lab in this manual assumes that the student servers are in their baseline configuration, as described in Lab 1-2 "Preparing an Application Server." If you have not done so already, complete the initial configuration tasks in Lab 1-2-1 before beginning this lab.

Your instructor should have supplied the information needed to complete the following table:

Student computer name (NT2670Srv##A)	
Student account name (Student##)	

To complete the exercises in this lab, you must access a second student computer on the classroom network, referred to in the exercises as your *partner server*. Depending on the network configuration, use one of the following options, as directed by your instructor:

- For a conventional classroom network with one operating system installed on each computer, your lab partner must perform the same exercises on his or her computer, known as your partner server.

- For a classroom in which each computer uses local virtualization software to install multiple operating systems, you must perform the exercises separately on two virtual machines representing your student server and your partner server.

- For a classroom using online virtualization, you must perform the exercises separately on two virtual student servers, representing your student server and your partner server, in your Web browser.

Working with Lab Worksheets

Each lab in this manual requires that you answer questions, save images of your screen, or perform other activities that you document in a worksheet named for the lab and task, such as *lab2_2_worksheet*. Your instructor provided you with lab worksheets. As you perform the tasks and exercises in each lab, open the appropriate worksheet file using WordPad, fill in the required information, and save the file to your computer's Student##\Documents folder. Print a copy for your instructor.

The procedure for opening and saving a worksheet file is as follows:

1. Open worksheet document opens in WordPad.

2. Complete all of the exercises in the worksheet.

3. In WordPad, choose Save As from the File menu. The Save As dialog box appears.

4. In the File Name text box, key **lab##_worksheet_*yourname*** (where lab##_task## contains the number of the lab and task you're completing, and *yourname* is your last name), and click Save.

5. Print a copy for your instructor.

SCENARIO

You are a new administrator for Contoso##, Ltd., working on a test deployment of the application server technologies included with Windows Server 2008. In this lab, you test the capabilities of the Web Server (IIS) role.

After completing this lab, you will be able to:

- Configure IIS7 properties at the server and site level
- Create Web sites
- Create virtual directories
- Configure site bindings

Exercise 2-2-1	Installing the Web Server (IIS) Role
Overview	In this exercise, you install IIS7 by adding the Web Server (IIS) role to the computer.
Completion time	5 minutes

1. Turn on your NT2670Srv##A computer. When the logon screen appears, log on using your *Administrator* account and the password *P@ssw0rd*.

2. If the Initial Configuration Tasks (ICT) screen window opens automatically, place a checkmark next to Do not show this window at logon, and click Close.

3. The Server Manager window will be displayed automatically. If the Server Manager window does not display automatically on NT2670Srv##A Click Start > Administrative Tools > Server Manager and start the Add Roles Wizard.

4. Click Next to bypass the *Before You Begin* page. The *Select Server Roles* page appears.

5. Select the Web Server (IIS) checkbox. An Add Roles Wizard message box appears, listing the features required to add the Web Server (IIS) role.

Question 1	*Why is the Windows Process Activation Services needed to run the Web Server (IIS) role?*

6. Click Add Required Features, and then click Next. The *Introduction To Web Server (IIS)* page appears.

7. Click Next to bypass the introductory page. The *Select Role Services* page appears.

8. Click Next to accept the default role service selections. The *Confirm Installation Selections* page appears.

9. Click Install. The wizard installs the role.

10. Click Close.

11. Close Server Manager, and leave the computer logged on for the next exercise.

Exercise 2-2-2	Configuring Web Server Properties
Overview	Using the default Web site that Windows Server 2008 creates during the role installation, experiment with the various IIS7 site display options.
Completion time	15 minutes

1. Click Start, and then click Internet Explorer. An Internet Explorer window appears.

> *If the default Internet Explorer page states that Internet Explorer Enhanced Security Configuration is enabled, open Server Manager. In the Server Summary box under Security Information, click Configure IE ESC, and turn ESC off for Administrators.*

2. In the Address box, key **http://127.0.0.1**, and press Enter. An IIS7 splash page appears.

> *A Microsoft Phishing Filter window may appear, select Turn off automatic Phishing Filter and click OK.*

3. Click Start. Then click Administrative Tools > Internet Information Services (IIS) Manager. The Internet Information Services (IIS) Manager window is displayed, shown in Figure 2-2-1.

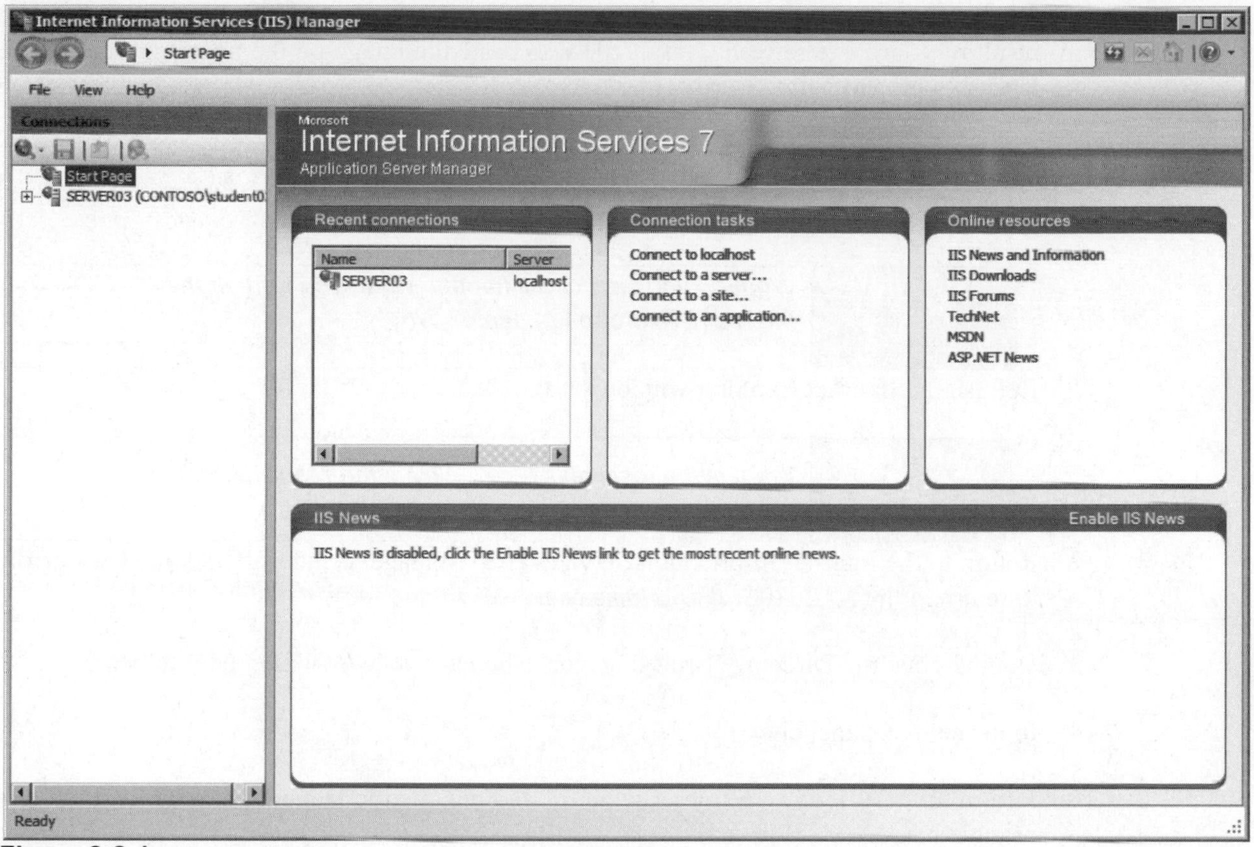

Figure 2-2-1
Internet Information Services (IIS) Manager window

4. Expand the NT2670Srv##A node representing your server. The NT2670Srv##A *Home* page appears in the middle pane.

5. Double-click the Default Document icon. The *Default Document* page appears in the middle pane.

6. Select the iisstart.htm file and, in the actions pane, click Remove. Then, click Yes to confirm the removal.

NOTE	*Removing a file from the Default Document page does not delete the file itself; it merely removes the file reference from the IIS7 configuration.*

7. Switch back to the Internet Explorer window, and click the Refresh button. An error message page appears, citing an HTTP Error 403.14.

Question 2	*What conclusion can you draw from this result?*

8. Press Ctrl+Prt Scr to take a screen shot of the Internet Explorer window showing the result of your page refresh. Press Ctrl+V to paste the image on the page provided in the lab2_2_worksheet file.

9. Open Windows Explorer, and browse to the C:\Inetpub\wwwroot folder.

10. Locate the iisstart file, and rename it **Default**.

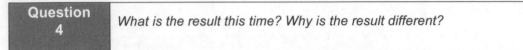

Question 3	What do you predict will happen when you refresh the Internet Explorer page again? Why?

11. Refresh the Internet Explorer window.

Question 4	What is the result this time? Why is the result different?

12. Return to the Internet Information Services (IIS) Manager window. Click the back arrow to return to the NT2670Srv##A *Home* page.

13. Double-click the Directory Browsing icon. The *Directory Browsing* page appears.

14. In the actions pane, click Enable.

15. Return to the Windows Explorer window, and rename the Default file **iisstart**, the file's original name.

16. Refresh the Internet Explorer window.

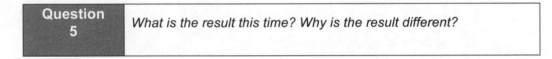

Question 5	What is the result this time? Why is the result different?

17. Press Ctrl+Prt Scr to take a screen shot of the Internet Explorer window showing the result of your page refresh. Press Ctrl+V to paste the image on the page provided in the lab2_2_worksheet file.

18. In the Internet Information Services (IIS) Manager window, disable the Directory Browsing option, and click the back arrow to return to the *NT2670Srv##A Home* page.

19. Double-click the Error Pages icon. The *Error Pages* page appears.

20. In the actions pane, click Edit Feature Settings. The Edit Error Pages Settings dialog box appears.

21. Select the Custom Error Pages option, and click OK.

22. Refresh the Internet Explorer window.

Question 6	*How is this error message page different from the previous one?*

23. Press Ctrl+Prt Scr to take a screen shot of the Internet Explorer window showing the result of your page refresh. Press Ctrl+V to paste the image on the page provided in the lab2_2_worksheet file.

24. Open the Edit Error Pages Settings dialog box again, and select the Detailed Errors For Local Requests And Custom Error Pages For Remote Requests option. Then click OK.

25. Click the back arrow to return to the NT2670Srv##A *Home* page.

26. Open the *Default Document* page again and, in the actions pane, click Add. The Add Default Document dialog box appears.

27. In the Name text box, key **iisstart.htm**, and click OK.

28. Click the back arrow to return to the NT2670Srv##A *Home* page.

29. Refresh the Internet Explorer window one last time. The IIS7 splash page appears again.

30. Leave the computer logged on for the next exercise.

Exercise 2-2-3   Preparing Web Site Content

Overview	Before you can create new Web sites on your IIS7 server, you must have content to publish on them.
Completion time	15 minutes

1. Click Start. Then click All Programs > Accessories > Notepad. A Notepad window appears.

2. In the Notepad window, key the following text, replacing the ## with the number assigned to your server.

    ```
    <html>

    <body>

    <h1 align="center">Contoso, LTD.</h2>

    <h2 align="center">www99.contoso99.com</h2>

    </body>

    </html>
    ```

3. Click File > Save As. The Save As dialog box appears.

4. Click Browse Folders. The dialog box expands to display the contents of your Documents folder.

5. Click New Folder. Then, key **www##**, where ## is the number assigned to your server, and press Enter.

6. In the Save As Type drop-down list, select All Files.

7. In the File Name text box, key **Default.htm**, and click Save.

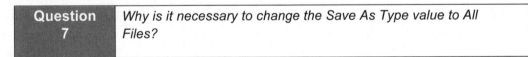

Question 7	*Why is it necessary to change the Save As Type value to All Files?*

8. Create another subfolder in your Documents folder called **Sales##**. Create a file inside it called **Default.htm**, containing the following text:

```
<html>

<body>

<h1 align="center">Contoso, LTD.</h2>

<h2 align="center">sales99.contoso99.com</h2>

</body>

</html>
```

9. Close the Notepad window.

10. Click Start. Then, click Administrative Tools > DNS.

11. Expand the NT2670Srv##A node and the Forward Lookup Zones folder.

12. Right-click the contoso##.com zone and, from the context menu, select New Alias (CNAME). The New Resource Record dialog box appears, as shown in Figure 2-2-2.

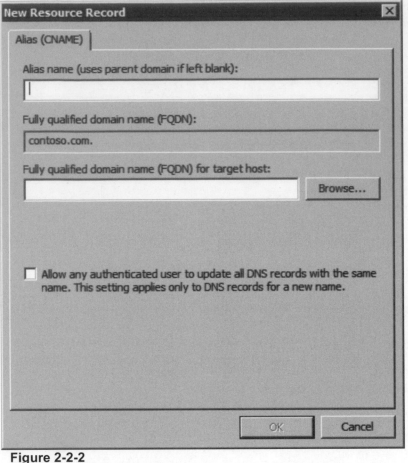

Figure 2-2-2
New Resource Record dialog box

13. In the Alias Name text box, key **www##**, where ## is the number assigned to your server.

14. In the Fully Qualified Domain Name (FQDN) For Target Host text box, key **NT2670Srv##A.contoso##.com**, where ## is the number assigned to your server. Then, click OK.

15. Repeat the process to create another New Alias (CNAME) record, using the alias name **sales##** and the target host name **NT2670Srv##A.contoso##.com**.

16. Press Ctrl+Prt Scr to take a screen shot of the DNS Manager console showing the two CNAME records you created. Pess Ctrl+V to paste the image on the page provided in the lab2_2_worksheet file.

17. Close the DNS Manager console, and leave the computer logged on for the next exercise.

Exercise 2-2-4   Creating Web Sites

Overview	To test IIS7's ability to support multiple Web sites simultaneously, create two new sites, and configure them to respond to different URLs.
Completion time	10 minutes

1.   Open the Internet Information Services (IIS) Manager window, and expand the Sites node.

2.   Right-click the Sites node and, from the context menu, select Add Web Site. The Add Web Site dialog box appears, as shown in Figure 2-2-3.

Figure 2-2-3
Add Web Site dialog box

3.   In the Site Name text box, key **www##**, where ## is the number assigned to your server.

4.   In the Physical Path text box, key or browse to the **C:\User\Administrator\Documents\www##** folder.

5. In the Add Web Site dialog box, key **www##.contoso##.com** in the Host Name text box, where ## is the number assigned to your server. Click the connect as button, select the Specific user option and click Set. Enter Administrator as the username and the password P@ssw0rd.

6. Click OK.

7. Create another Web site using the following settings:

    • Site Name: sales##

    • Physical Path: C:\Users\Student##\Documents\sales##

    • User Name: Administrator

    • Password: P@ssw0rd

    • Host Name: sales##.contoso##.com

8. Press Ctrl+Prt Scr to take a screen shot of the Internet Information Services (IIS) Manager window showing the two Web sites you created. Press Ctrl+V to paste the image on the page provided in the lab2_2_worksheet file.

9. In Internet Explorer, key **http://www##.contoso##.com** in the address box, and press Enter.

Question 8	What happens?

10. Press Ctrl+Prt Scr to take a screen shot of the Internet Explorer window. Press Ctrl+V to paste the image on the page provided in the lab2_2_worksheet file.

11. Key **http://sales##.contoso##.com** in the address box, and press Enter.

Question 9	What happens now?
Question 10	How is IIS7 able to distinguish between the two URLs when the www##￼ and sales## names resolve to the same IP address?
Question 11	Which Web page appears when you key the URL http://NT2670Srv##A.contoso##.com? Why?
Question 12	Which Web page appears when you key a URL containing the server's IP address instead of a name? Why?

12. Leave the computer logged on for the next exercise.

Exercise 2-2-5   Creating Virtual Directories

Overview	In this exercise, use virtual directories to publish content found at a different location as part of an existing Web site.
Completion time	15 minutes

1. Open Windows Explorer, and browse to the Documents\www## folder you created in Exercise 2-2-3.

2. In the www## folder, create a subfolder called **Public**.

3. In the Public folder, use Notepad to create a file called **Default.htm** that contains the following text:

   ```
   <html>

   <body>

   <h1 align="center">Contoso, LTD.</h2>

   <h2 align="center">Public</h2>

   </body>

   </html>
   ```

4. In Internet Explorer, key **http://www##.contoso##.com/public** in the address box, and press Enter. The Public page you created appears.

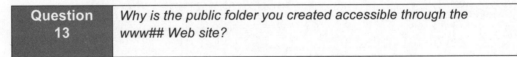

Question 13	*Why is the public folder you created accessible through the www## Web site?*

5. In the Internet Information Services (IIS) Manager window, right-click the www## site you created in Exercise 2-2-4 and, from the context menu, select Add Virtual Directory. The Add Virtual Directory dialog box appears, as shown in Figure 2-2-4.

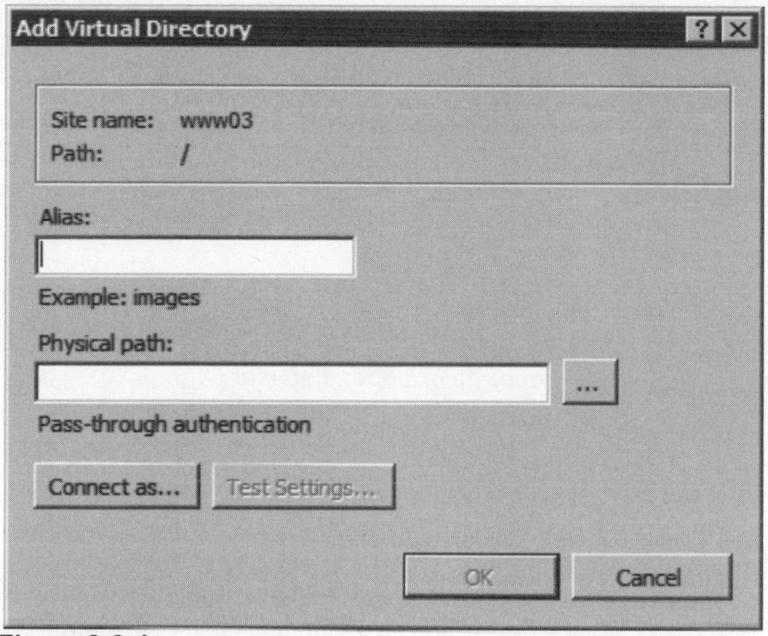

Figure 2-2-4
Add Virtual Directory dialog box

6. In the Alias text box, key **Links**.

7. In the Physical Path text box, key or browse to the **C:\Users\Administrator\Links** folder, where ## is the number assigned to your computer.

8. Click Test Settings. The Test Connection dialog box appears.

Question 14	What are the results of the authentication and authorization tests? Explain the results.

9. Click Close. The Test Connection dialog box closes.

10. In the Add Virtual Directory text box, click Connect As. The Connect As dialog box appears.

11. Select the Specific User option, and click Set. The Set Credentials dialog box appears.

12. In the User Name text box, key **contoso##\Administrator,** where ## is the number assigned to your server.

13. In the Password and Confirm Password text boxes, key **P@ssw0rd**. Then click OK.

14. Click OK to close the Connect As dialog box.

15. Click Test Settings again.

Question 15	What are the results now?
Question 16	What URL must you use in Internet Explorer to access the virtual directory you just created?

16. In Internet Explorer, key the URL for the Links virtual directory, and press Enter.

Question 17	Why does an error page appear?

17. In the Internet Information Services (IIS) Manager window, select the www## site. The *www## Home* Web page appears.

18. Double-click the Directory Browsing icon, and enable directory browsing.

19. Switch to Internet Explorer, and click the Refresh button.

Question 18	What is the result?

20. Create an identical Links virtual directory on your sales## site, and attempt to access it using Internet Explorer.

21. In the Internet Information Services (IIS) Manager window, with the www## site selected, click the Content View tab.

22. Press Ctrl+Prt Scr to take a screen shot of the Internet Information Services (IIS) Manager window. Press Ctrl+V to paste the image on the page provided in the lab2_2_worksheet file.

23. Close all open windows, and log off of both computers.

LAB REVIEW: QUESTIONS

Completion time	5 minutes

1. In Exercise 2-2-2, you saw the two different types of error pages that IIS7 can generate. By default, the Web server displays detailed error pages in response to local requests and the simple error pages in response to remote requests. What is the main reason for providing less error information to remote users?

2. In Exercise 2-2-3, you created two CNAME resource records in your domain using the DNS Manager console. Why was it necessary to create these records?

3. In Exercise 2-2-3, why did you create CNAME resource records instead of standard Host (A) records in the DNS?

4. In Exercise 2-2-4, you configure your two new Web sites to use host name bindings. Why is this binding method preferable to using a different port number for each site?

LAB CHALLENGE: CREATING PORT NUMBER BINDINGS

Completion time	20 minutes

Your supervisor wants you to experiment with the different site binding strategies supported by IIS7. To complete this challenge, create a Web site called **testsite##**, containing the same type of dummy content you used earlier in this lab. The Web site must be accessible using any of the following URLs, where ## is replaced with the number assigned to your computer:

> http://server##.contoso##.com:1024
>
> http://testsite##.contoso##.com
>
> http://testsite##.contoso##.com:1025
>
> http://testsite##.contoso##.com
>
> http://testsite##.contoso##.com:1026

Create a list of the tasks you must perform to achieve your goal, and take five separate screen shots of the Internet Explorer window, displaying each of the five URLs successfully connected to the site. Paste the images in the lab2_2_worksheet file.

LAB 3-1 70-643
CONFIGURING IIS7

This lab contains the following exercises:

Exercise 3-1-1 Installing the Web Server (IIS) Role
Exercise 3-1-2 Configuring IP Address Restrictions
Exercise 3-1-3 Configuring Anonymous Authentication
Exercise 3-1-4 Using Basic and Windows Authentication
Exercise 3-1-5 Configuring SSL
Lab Review: Questions
Lab Challenge: Building a Secure Website

Estimated lab time: 80 minutes

BEFORE YOU BEGIN

The classroom network consists of Windows Server 2008 student server A and B a connected to via an internal local area network. NT2670Srv##A the domain controller for the contoso.com domain, is running Windows Server 2008. Throughout the labs in this manual, you will install, configure, maintain, and troubleshoot application roles, features, and services on the NT2670Srv##A.

To accommodate various types of classroom arrangements, each lab in this manual assumes that the student servers are in their baseline configuration, as described in Lab 1-2 "Preparing an Application Server." If you have not done so already, complete the initial configuration tasks in Lab 1-2-1 before beginning this lab.

Your instructor should have supplied the information needed to complete the following table:

Student computer name (NT2670Srv##A)	
Student account name (Student##)	

To complete the exercises in this lab, you must access a second student computer on the classroom network, referred to in the exercises as your *partner server*. Depending on the network configuration, use one of the following options, as directed by your instructor:

- For a conventional classroom network with one operating system installed on each computer, your lab partner must perform the same exercises on his or her computer, known as your partner server.

- For a classroom in which each computer uses local virtualization software to install multiple operating systems, you must perform the exercises separately on two virtual machines representing your student server and your partner server.

- For a classroom using online virtualization, you must perform the exercises separately on two virtual student servers, representing your student server and your partner server, in your Web browser.

Working with Lab Worksheets

Each lab in this manual requires that you answer questions, save images of your screen, or perform other activities that you document in a worksheet named for the lab and task, such as *lab3_1_ worksheet*. Your instructor provided you with lab worksheets. As you perform the tasks and exercises in each lab, open the appropriate worksheet file using WordPad, fill in the required information, and save the file to your computer's Student##\Documents folder. Print a copy for your instructor.

The procedure for opening and saving a worksheet file is as follows:

1. Open worksheet document opens in WordPad.

2. Complete all of the exercises in the worksheet.

3. In WordPad, choose Save As from the File menu. The Save As dialog box appears.

4. In the File Name text box, key **lab##_ worksheet_*yourname*** (where lab##_*task##* contains the number of the lab and task you're completing, and *yourname* is your last name), and click Save.

5. Print a copy for your instructor.

SCENARIO

You are a new administrator for Contoso##, Ltd., working on a test deployment of the application server technologies included with Windows Server 2008. In this lab, you test the security capabilities of the Web Server (IIS) role.

After completing this lab, you will be able to:

- Configure IP address restrictions

- Configure Web site authentication methods

- Secure a Web site with SSL

Exercise 3-1-1	Installing the Web Server (IIS) Role (DO NOT DO IF IIS IS ALREADY INSTALLED)
Overview	In this exercise, install IIS7 by adding the Web Server (IIS) role to the computer.
Completion time	5 minutes

1. Turn on your NT2670Srv##A and NT2670Srv##B computers. On the NT2670Srv##A computer, when the logon screen appears, log on using your *Administrator* account and the password *P@ssw0rd*. If the Initial Configuration screen appears, close it.

2. The Server Manager console appears. If the Server Manager console does not appear; click Start > Administrative Tools > Server Manager. In the Server Manager scope pane, select the Roles node, and then click Add Roles.

3. Click Next to bypass the *Before You Begin* page. The *Select Server Roles* page appears.

> **NOTE**
> *If your computer already has the Web Server (IIS) role installed with its default selection of role services, you can proceed immediately to Exercise 3-1-2. The sites and configuration settings you created will not interfere with the completion of the Lab 3-1.*

4. Select the Web Server (IIS) checkbox, and click Next. An Add Roles Wizard message box appears, listing the features required to add the Web Server (IIS) role.

5. Click Add Required Features, and then click Next. The *Introduction To Web Server (IIS)* page appears.

6. Click Next to bypass the introductory page. The *Select Role Services* page appears.

7. Click Next to accept the default role service selections. The *Confirm Installation Selections* page appears.

8. Click Install. The wizard installs the role.

9. Click Close.

10. Close Server Manager, and leave the computer logged on for the next exercise.

Exercise 3-1-2   Configuring IP Address Restrictions

Overview	In this exercise, you control access to a Web site based on the IP addresses of the client computers.
Completion time	15 minutes

1. Turn on your NT2670Srv##A and NT2670Srv##B computers. On the NT2670Srv##A computer, when the logon screen appears, log on using your *Administrator* account and the password *P@ssw0rd*. If the Initial Configuration screen appears, close it.

2. The Server Manager console appears. If the Server Manager console does not appear; click Start > Administrative Tools > Server Manager. In the Server Manager scope pane, select the Roles node in the scope (left) pane.

3. In the detail (right) pane under roles click the Web Server (IIS) hyperlink, on the Web server (IIS) page click Add Role Services. The Add Role Services wizard appears, displaying the *Select Role Services* page.

4. Select the Security > IP and Domain Restrictions checkbox, and click Next. The *Confirm Installation Selections* page appears.

5. Click Install. The wizard installs the role service, and the *Installation Results* page appears.

6. Click Close.

7. Open Internet Explorer. In the address box, key **http://127.0.0.1**, and press Enter.

Question 1	What happens?

8. On the NT2670Srv##B computer, log on using your *Administrator* account and the password *P@ssw0rd*. If the Initial Configuration screen appears, close it and also close Server Manager if it appears. Open Internet Explorer, and try to connect to the following URL: **http://NT2670##A.contoso##.com**.

Question 2	What is the result?
Question 3	What can you infer from these results about the default settings of the IP and Domain Restrictions role service?

9. On the NT2670Srv##A computer, open the Internet Information Services (IIS) Manager window, and expand the NT2670Srv##A and Sites nodes.

10. Select Default Web Site. The *Default Web Site* home page appears.

11. Double-click the IPv4 Address and Domain Restrictions icon. The *IPv4 Address And Domain Restrictions* page appears, as shown in Figure 3-1-1.

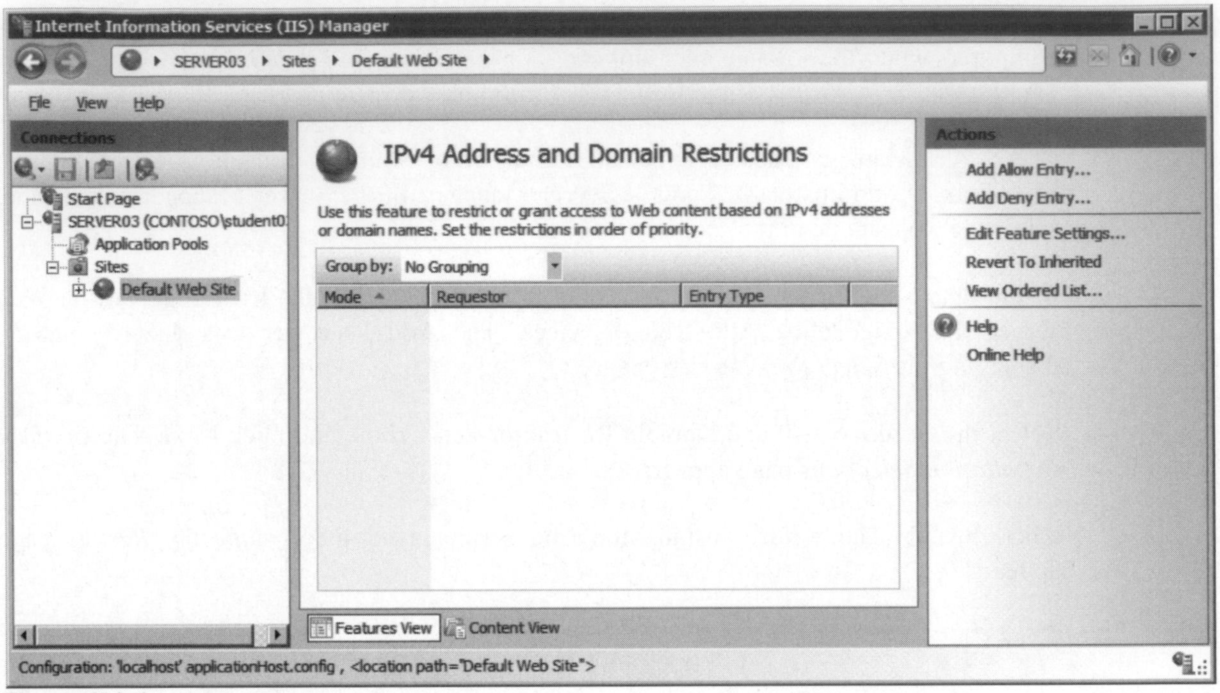

Figure 3-1-1
IPv4 Address And Domain Restrictions page

12. In the actions pane, click Edit Feature Settings. The Edit IP And Domain Restrictions Settings dialog box appears.

13. From the Access For Unspecified Clients drop-down list, select Deny, and click OK.

14. Switch to Internet Explorer, and click the Refresh button.

Question 4	What happens?

15. On the NT2670Srv##B computer, in Internet Explorer, try again to connect to http://NT2670Srv##A.contoso##.com.

Question 5	*What is the result?*

16. In the Internet Information Services (IIS) Manager window, in the actions pane, click Add Allow Entry. The Add Allow Restriction Rule dialog box appears, as shown in Figure 3-1-2.

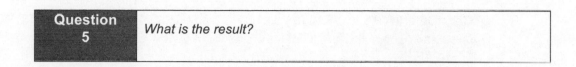

Figure 3-1-2
Add Allow Restriction Rule dialog box

17. Leave the Specific IPv4 Address option selected. In the text box, key **127.0.0.1**, and click OK. The new rule you created appears in the IPv4 Address And Domain Restrictions list.

18. Switch to Internet Explorer, and click the Refresh button.

Question 6	*What happens?*

19. On the NT2670Srv##B computer, switch to Internet Explorer, and try again to connect to the **http://NT2670Srv##A.contoso##.com** URL.

Question 7	What is the result?
Question 8	Why can you connect to the Web site from one computer and not from the other?

20. On the NT2670Srv##B computer, click Start. Then click All Programs > Accessories > Command Prompt. A command-prompt window appears.

21. In the command-prompt window, key **ipconfig /all**, and press Enter.

22. Key the computer name and IP address assigned to the NT2670Srv##B computer in the following table.

Computer Name	IP Address

23. Back on the NT2670Srv##A computer, create a new Allow entry for the NT2670Srv##B computer's IP address.

24. Retest your access to the Web site from both computers, just as you did in steps 18 to 19.

Question 9	What are the results?
Question 10	If you try connecting to your Web site from a network computer other than your server or your partner server, what would be the result? Why?

25. On the NT2670##A computer, In the Internet Information Services (IIS) Manager window, in the actions pane, click Add Allow Entry. The Add Allow Restriction Rule dialog box appears.

26. Select the IPv4 Address Range option and, in the text box, key **172.16.##.0**.

27. In the Mask text box, key **255.255.255.0**, and click OK. The new rule you created appears in the IPv4 Address And Domain Restrictions list.

28. Press Ctrl+Prt Scr to take a screen shot of the Internet Information Services (IIS) Manager window showing the three rules you created. Press Ctrl+V to paste the image on the page provided in the lab3_1_worksheet file.

29. Click Edit Feature Settings again, and select Allow from the Access For Unspecified Clients drop-down list. Then, click OK.

30. Leave both computers logged on for the next exercise.

Exercise 3-1-3   Configuring Anonymous Authentication

Overview	In this exercise, configure the properties of IIS7's Anonymous Authentication module.
Completion time	15 minutes

1. On the NT2670Srv##A computer, click Start. Then click Administrative Tools > Active Directory Users And Computers. The Active Directory Users And Computers console appears, as shown in Figure 3-1-3.

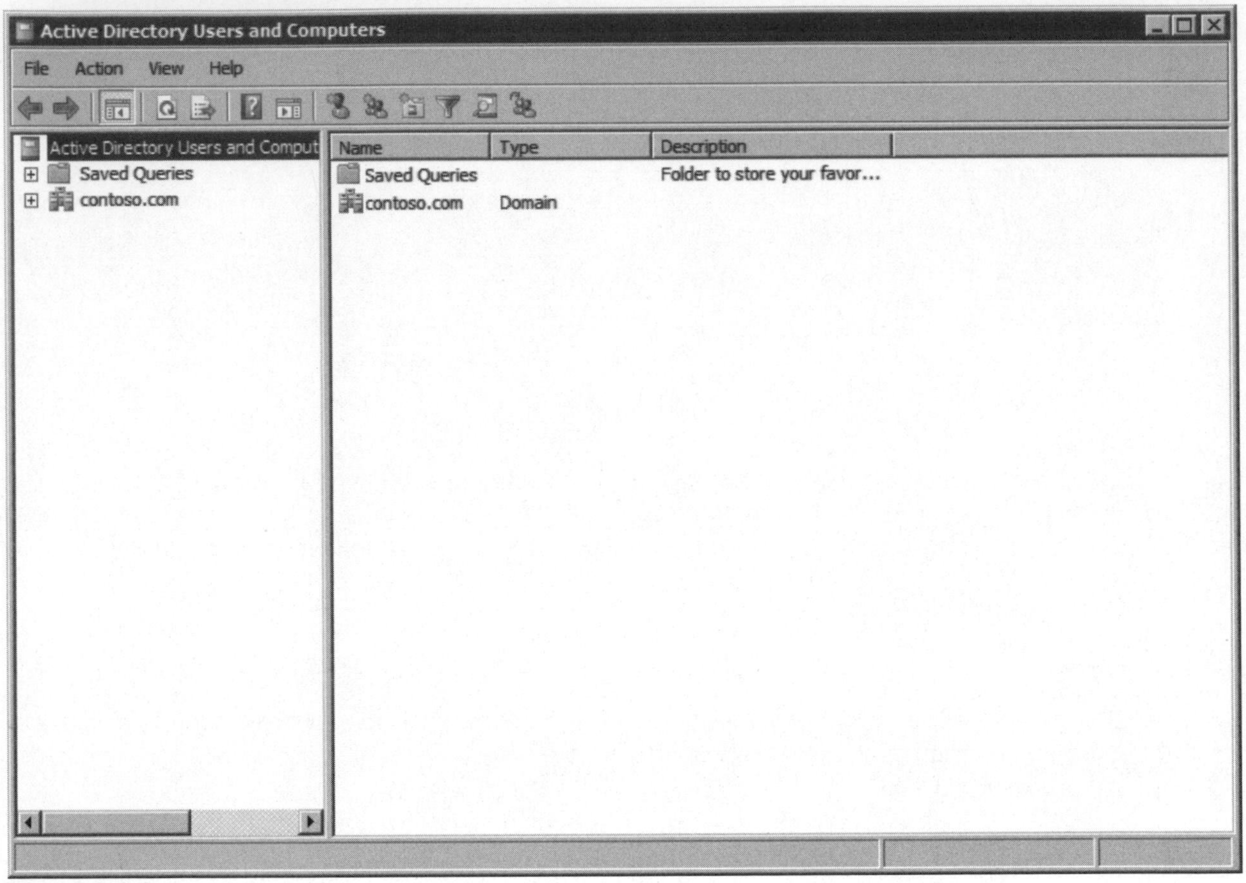

Figure 3-1-3
Active Directory Users And Computers console

2. In the Users container, create a new user account with the following properties:

    - First Name: IUSR##, where ## is the number assigned to your computer

    - User Logon Name: IUSR##

    - Password: P@ssw0rd

    - Clear the User Must Change Password At Next Logon checkbox

    - Select the Password Never Expires checkbox

3. Open the Properties sheet for the user account you just created, and click the Member Of tab.

4. Add the user to the IIS_IUSRS group, and click OK to close the Properties sheet.

NOTE	*To review the steps for creating and managing domain user accounts, see Optional Review Exercise: Testing Share Access at the end of Lab 3-1.*

5. In the Internet Information Services (IIS) Manager window, select Default Web Site.

6. Double-click the Authentication icon. The Authentication page appears.

Question 11	*What authentication methods are provided in the default IIS7 configuration?*

7. In the list of authentication methods, select Anonymous Authentication. Then, in the actions pane, click Edit. The Edit Anonymous Authentication Credentials dialog box appears.

Question 12	*What anonymous user identity is IIS7 currently using?*

8. Click Set. The Set Credentials dialog box appears.

9. In the User Name text box, key **contoso##\IUSR##**, where ## is the number assigned to your computer.

10. In the Password and Confirm Password text boxes, key **P@ssw0rd**.

11. Click OK to close the Set Credentials dialog box.

12. Click OK to close the Edit Anonymous Authentication Credentials dialog box.

13. In the Active Directory Users And Computers console, right-click the IUSR## object and, from the context menu, select Disable Account. An Active Directory Domain Services message box appears, informing you that the account is disabled.

14. Click OK.

15. Close all open windows, and restart the computer. Then, log on using your Administrator account and the password P@ssw0rd.

16. Open Internet Explorer, and try to connect to the URL http://127.0.0.1.

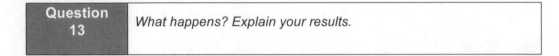

Question 13	What happens? Explain your results.

17. Press Ctrl+Prt Scr to take a screen shot of the Internet Explorer window. Press Ctrl+V to paste the image on the page provided in the lab3_1_worksheet file.

18. Open the Active Directory Users And Computers console, right-click the IUSR## account you created and, on the context menu, click Enable Account.

19. Open the Internet Information Services (IIS) Manager window, select Default Web Site and, in the actions pane, click Restart.

20. Switch to Internet Explorer, and click the Refresh button.

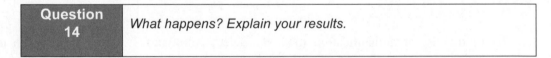

Question 14	What happens? Explain your results.

21. Close Internet Explorer and the Internet Information Services (IIS) Manager window, and leave the computer logged on for the next exercise.

Exercise 3-1-4	Using Basic and Windows Authentication
Overview	In this exercise, install the Basic and Windows Authentication modules, and configure an IIS7 Web site to use them.
Completion time	10 minutes

1. On the NT2670Srv##A computer, open Server Manager, and select the Roles node in the scope (left) pane.

2. In the detail (right) pane under roles click the Web Server (IIS) hyperlink, on the Web server (IIS) page click Add Role Services. The Add Role Services wizard appears, displaying the *Select Role Services* page.

3. Select the following role services, and click Next. The *Confirm Installation Selections* page appears.

    *   Security > Basic Authentication

    *   Security > Windows Authentication

    *   Security > Digest Authentication

4. Click Install. The wizard installs the role service, and the *Installation Results* page appears.

5. Click Close.

6. Open the Internet Information Services (IIS) Manager window, select Default Web Site, and double-click the Authentication icon. The *Authentication* home page appears, as shown in Figure 3-1-4.

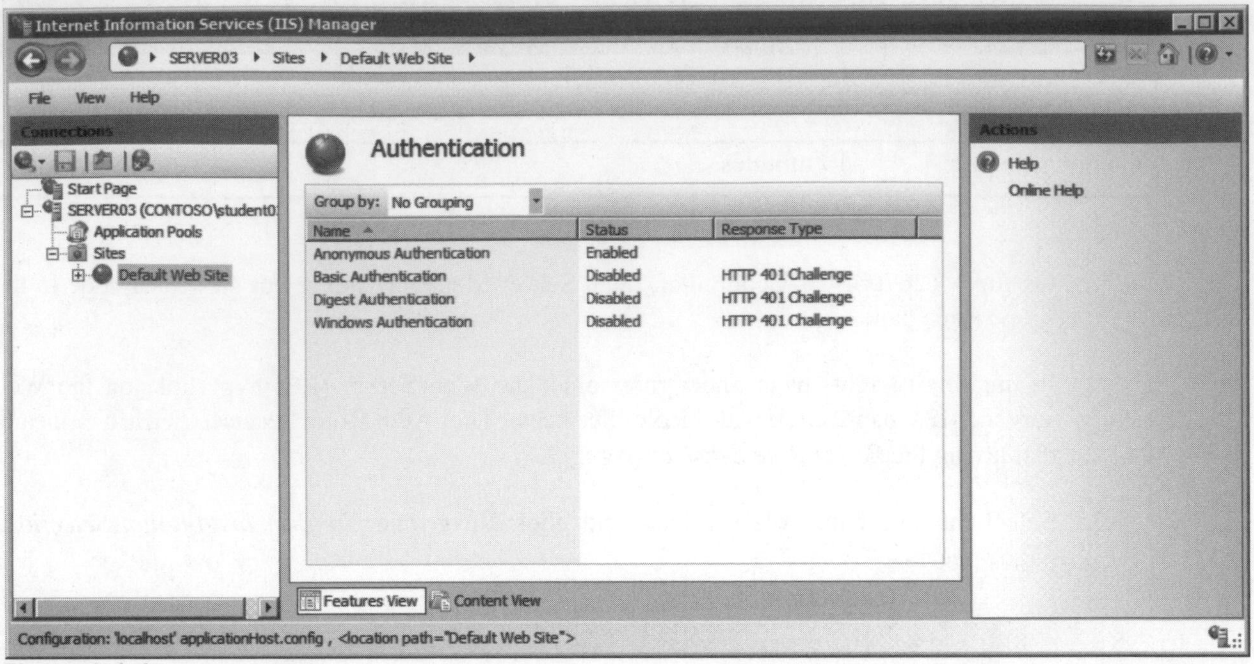

Figure 3-1-4
Authentication home page

Question 15	Which of the installed authentication modules is currently enabled?

7. Select Basic Authentication and, in the actions menu, select Enable.

8. Open Internet Explorer and, in the address box, key **http://NT2670Srv##A.contoso##.com**, where ## is the number assigned to your computer, and press Enter.

Question 16	What happens?
Question 17	Which authentication method is Internet Explorer currently using? How can you tell?

9. In the Internet Information Services (IIS) Manager window, select Anonymous Authentication and, in the actions pane, select Disable.

10. Switch to Internet Explorer, and click the Refresh button.

Question 18	*What happens?*
Question 19	*Which authentication method is Internet Explorer using now? How can you tell?*

11. In the User Name text box, key **Student4**. In the Password text box, key **P@ssw0rd**. Then click OK.

Question 20	*What happens?*

12. Try to log on two more times by entering the same credentials and clicking OK.

Question 21	*What happens after three failed logon attempts?*

13. Press Ctrl+Prt Scr to take a screen shot of the Internet Explorer window. Press Ctrl+V to paste the image on the page provided in the lab3_1_worksheet file.

14. In Internet Explorer, click the Refresh button, and try to log on with the user name *contoso##\Student##* and the password *P@ssw0rd*.

Question 22	*What happens now?*

15. Close all Internet Explorer windows.

16. In the Internet Information Services (IIS) Manager window, select Windows Authentication and, in the actions pane, select Enable.

17. Open Internet Explorer, and connect again to http://NT2670Srv##A.contoso##.com, where ## is the number assigned to your computer.

18. Log on with the user name *contoso##\Student##* and the password *P@ssw0rd*.

Question 23	What is the result?
Question 24	Which authentication method did Internet Explorer use to connect to the site? How can you tell?

19. Close all Internet Explorer windows.

20. In the Internet Information Services (IIS) Manager window, enable Anonymous Authentication, and disable Basic Authentication and Windows Authentication.

21. Leave the computer logged on for the next exercise.

Exercise 3-1-5   Configuring SSL

Overview	In this exercise, configure a Web site to use SSL encryption.
Completion time	10 minutes

1. On the NT2670Srv##A computer, in the Internet Information Services (IIS) Manager window, select the NT2670Srv##A node, and double-click the Server Certificates icon. The *Server Certificates* page appears, as shown in Figure 3-1-5.

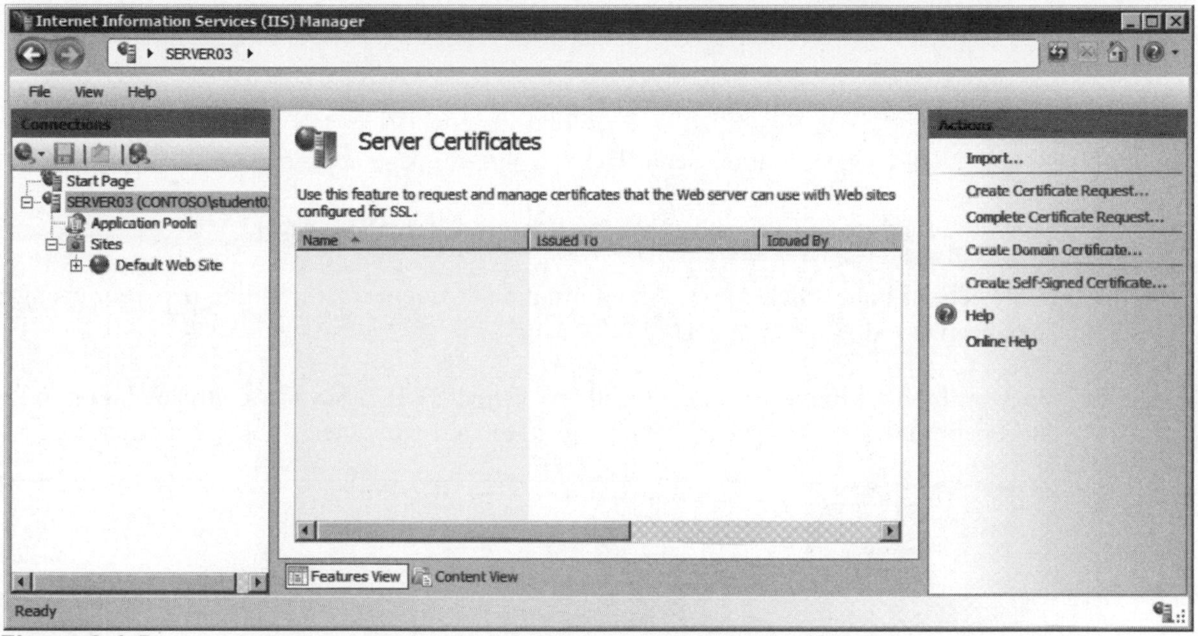

Figure 3-1-5
Server Certificates page in the Internet Information Services (IIS) Manager window

2. In the actions pane, click Create Self-Signed Certificate. The Create Self-Signed Certificate dialog box appears.

3. In the Specify A Friendly Name For the Certificate text box, key **NT2670Srv##A**, where ## is the number assigned to your computer, and click OK. A new certificate appears in the Server Certificates list.

4. In the actions pane, click View. A Certificate dialog box appears.

5. Press Ctrl+Prt Scr to take a screen shot of the Certificate dialog box. Press Ctrl+V to paste the image on the page provided in the lab3_1_worksheet file.

6. Click OK to close the Certificate dialog box.

7. In the Internet Information Services (IIS) Manager window, select Default Web Site and, in the actions pane, click Bindings. The Site Bindings dialog box appears.

8. Click Add. The Add Site Binding dialog box appears.

9. In the Type dropdown list, select https.

10. In the SSL Certificate dropdown list, select NT2670Srv##A.

11. Click OK. The new binding appears in the Site Bindings dialog box.

Question 25	Why are the two bindings listed in the Site Bindings box able to co-exist?

12. Click Close to close the Site Bindings dialog box.

13. Double-click the SSL Settings icon. The *SSL Settings* page appears.

14. Select the Require SSL checkbox and the Require 128-bit SSL checkbox.

15. In the actions pane, click Apply. An information box appears, indicating that your changes have been saved.

16. Open an Internet Explorer window, and key **http://NT2670Srv##A.contoso##.com** in the address box, where ## is the number assigned to your computer. Then press Enter.

Question 26	What happens?

17. Press Ctrl+Prt Scr to take a screen shot of the Internet Explorer window. Press Ctrl+V to paste the image on the page provided in the lab3_1_worksheet file.

18. Key **https://NT2670Srv##A.contoso##.com** in the address box, and press Enter. (If a Security Alert message box appears, click OK to continue.)

Question 27	What happens now?

19. On the NT2670Srv##B computer, open an Internet Explorer window, and try to connect to your server using the same https://NT2670Srv##A.contoso##.com URL. A *Certificate Error* page appears.

Question 28	Why does the Web site fail to load from your partner server when it loaded successfully from your server?

20. Close the Internet Explorer window.

21. Close all open windows, and log off both computers.

LAB REVIEW: QUESTIONS

Completion time	5 minutes

1. With the IP Address and Domain Restrictions settings configuration at the end of Exercise 3-1-2, would classroom computers other than your server and your partner server be able to access your Web site? Explain why or why not.

2. In Exercise 3-1-4, your repeated attempts to log on to your Web site using the *Student##* user name failed, but the logon was successful when you used the name *contoso##\Student##*. Explain why.

3. In Exercise 3-1-4, why was it necessary to shut down Internet Explorer and then restart it before logging on with Windows Authentication?

LAB CHALLENGE: BUILDING A SECURE WEB SITE

Completion time	20 minutes

Your supervisor wants you create a test Web site, using all of the security mechanisms you tested. To complete this challenge, create a new Web site named SecureSite on your server. Make it accessible using the URL https://securesite.contoso##.com. The site must adhere to the following requirements:

- The root directory must be accessible using Anonymous Authentication.

- Three subdirectories, called Tom, Dick, and Harry, must be accessible using only Basic Authentication.

- One virtual directory called Student##, pointing to the C:\Users\Student## folder, must be accessible using only Windows Authentication.

- The subdirectories and the virtual directory must be accessible only to users on the 10.1.1.0 network.

- The entire site must be secured using SSL with a self-signed certificate called SecureSite.

Take a screen shot of an Internet Explorer window showing the content of the Web site you created. Paste the image on the page provided in the lab3_1_worksheet file.

Take a screen shot of an Internet Explorer window showing the content of the virtual directory you created. Paste the image on the page provided in the lab3_1_worksheet file.

Optional Review Exercise	Testing Share Access
Overview	Create a test user account, and connect to the share from another computer on the network.
Completion time	15 minutes

1. Click Start, and then click Administrative Tools > Active Directory Users And Computers. In the User Account Control message box, click Continue to display the Active Directory Users and Computers console.

2. Expand the contoso.com domain, and select the Users container, as shown in Figure Review.1.

Figure Review.1
Active Directory Users And Computers Console

3. Right-click the Users container and, on the context menu, click New > User. The New Object – User wizard appears.

4. In the First Name and User Logon Name text boxes, key **User##**, where ## is the number assigned to your computer.

5. Click Next. On the next page, key **P@ssw0rd** in the Password and Confirm Password text boxes.

6. Clear the User Must Change Password At Next Logon checkbox, and select the Password Never Expires checkbox. Click Next.

7. Click Finish to create the new user object.

8. Right-click the Users container and, on the context menu, click New > Group. The New Object – Group wizard appears.

9. In the Group Name text box, key **Group##**, where ## is the number assigned to your computer.

10. Click OK to create the new group object.

11. In the Users container, double-click the User## object you created. The User## Properties sheet appears.

12. Click the Member Of tab.

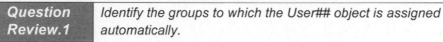

Question Review.1	Identify the groups to which the User## object is assigned automatically.

13. Click Add. The Select Groups dialog box appears.

14. In the Enter The Object Names To Select text box, key **Group##**. Click OK. Group## is added to the Member Of list.

15. Press Ctrl+Prt Scr to take a screen shot of the Member Of tab on the User## Properties sheet. Press Ctrl+V to paste the image on the page provided in the lab3_1_worksheet file.

16. Click OK to close the User## Properties sheet.

17. Move to your partner server on the classroom network, and log on to the domain with the User## account you created and the password P@ssw0rd.

NOTE	In a virtual machine environment, use a different virtual machine on your computer.

LAB 4-1 70-643
DEPLOYING AN FTP SERVER

This lab contains the following exercises:

Exercise 4-1-1 Installing the Web Server (IIS) Role
Exercise 4-1-2 Creating an FTP6 Site
Exercise 4-1-3 Configuring FTP6 Security
Lab Review. Questions
Lab Challenge: Creating a Combined Web/FTP Site

Estimated lab time: 55 minutes

BEFORE YOU BEGIN

The classroom network consists of Windows Server 2008 student server A and B a connected to via an internal local area network. NT2670Srv##A the domain controller for the contoso##.com domain, is running Windows Server 2008. Throughout the labs in this manual, you will install, configure, maintain, and troubleshoot application roles, features, and services on the NT2670Srv##A.

To accommodate various types of classroom arrangements, each lab in this manual assumes that the student servers are in their baseline configuration, as described in Lab 1-2, "Preparing an Application Server." If you have not done so already, complete the initial configuration tasks in Lab 1-2-1 before beginning this lab.

Your instructor should have supplied the information needed to complete the following table:

Student computer name (NT2670Srv##A)	
Student account name (Student##)	

To complete the exercises in this lab, you must access a second student computer on the classroom network, referred to in the exercises as your *partner server*. Depending on the network configuration, use one of the following options, as directed by your instructor:

- For a conventional classroom network with one operating system installed on each computer, your lab partner must perform the same exercises on his or her computer, known as your partner server.

- For a classroom in which each computer uses local virtualization software to install multiple operating systems, you must perform the exercises separately on two virtual machines representing your student server and your partner server.

- For a classroom using online virtualization, you must perform the exercises separately on two virtual student servers, representing your student server and your partner server, in your Web browser.

Working with Lab Worksheets

Each lab in this manual requires that you answer questions, save images of your screen, or perform other activities that you document in a worksheet named for the lab and task, such as *lab4_1_worksheet*. Your instructor provided you with lab worksheets. As you perform the tasks and exercises in each lab, open the appropriate worksheet file using WordPad, fill in the required information, and save the file to your computer's Student##\Documents folder. Print a copy for your instructor.

The procedure for opening and saving a worksheet file is as follows:

1. Open worksheet document opens in WordPad.

2. Complete all of the exercises in the worksheet.

3. In WordPad, choose Save As from the File menu. The Save As dialog box appears.

4. In the File Name text box, key **lab##_ worksheet_*yourname*** (where lab##_*task##* contains the number of the lab and task you're completing, and *yourname* is your last name), and click Save.

5. Print a copy for your instructor.

SCENARIO

You are a new administrator for Contoso##, Ltd., working on a test deployment of the application server technologies included with Windows Server 2008. In this lab, you compare the capabilities of the FTP Publishing Service role service included with Windows Server 2008 and the Microsoft FTP Service for IIS 7.0 module, which is available as a free download.

After completing this lab, you will be able to:

- Create FTP sites
- Configure FTP security components
- Create FTP virtual directories

Exercise 4-1-1	Installing the Web Server (IIS) Role (DO NOT DO IF IIS IS ALREADY INSTALLED)
Overview	In this exercise, install IIS7 by adding the Web Server (IIS) role to the computer.
Completion time	5 minutes

1. Turn on your NT2670Srv##A and NT2670Srv##B computers. On the NT2670Srv##A computer, when the logon screen appears, log on using your *Administrator* account and the password *P@ssw0rd*. If the Initial Configuration screen appears, close it.

2. The Server Manager console appears. If the Server Manager console does not appear; click Start > Administrative Tools > Server Manager. In the Server Manager scope pane, select the Roles node, and then click Add Roles.

3. Click Next to bypass the *Before You Begin* page. The *Select Server Roles* page appears.

> **NOTE**
> *If your computer already has the Web Server (IIS) role installed with its default selection of role services, you can proceed immediately to Exercise 4-1-2. The sites and configuration settings you created will not interfere with the completion of the Lab 4-1.*

4. Select the Web Server (IIS) checkbox, and click Next. An Add Roles Wizard message box appears, listing the features required to add the Web Server (IIS) role.

5. Click Add Required Features, and then click Next. The *Introduction to Web Server (IIS)* page appears.

6. Click Next to bypass the introductory page. The *Select Role Services* page appears.

7. Click Next to accept the default role service selections. The *Confirm Installation Selections* page appears.

8. Click Install. The wizard installs the role.

9. Click Close.

10. Close Server Manager, and leave the computer logged on for the next exercise.

Exercise 4-1-2	Creating an FTP6 Site
Overview	In this exercise, install the FTP Publishing Service role service, which provides basic FTP site hosting capabilities, and create a site.
Completion time	15 minutes

1. Turn on your NT2670Srv##A and NT2670Srv##B computers. On the NT2670Srv##A computer, when the logon screen appears, log on using your *Administrator* account and the password *P@ssw0rd*. If the Initial Configuration screen appears, close it.

2. The Server Manager console appears. If the Server Manager console does not appear; click Start > Administrative Tools > Server Manager. In the Server Manager scope pane, select the Roles node in the scope (left) pane.

3. In the detail (right) pane under roles click the Web Server (IIS) hyperlink, on the Web server (IIS) page click Add Role Services. The Add Role Services wizard appears, displaying the *Select Role Services* page.

4. Select the FTP Publishing Service checkbox. An Add Role Services Required For FTP Publishing Service dialog box appears, prompting you to install the IIS 6 Metabase Compatibility role service.

5. Click Add Required Role Services, and then click Next. The *Confirm Installation Selections* page appears.

6. Click Install. The wizard installs the role services, and the *Installation Results* page appears.

7. Click Close.

8. Click Start, and then click Administrative Tools > Internet Information Services (IIS) 6.0 Manager, the Internet Information Services (IIS) 6.0 Manager console appears.

9. Expand the NT2670Srv##A node and the FTP Sites folder, as shown in Figure 4-1-1.

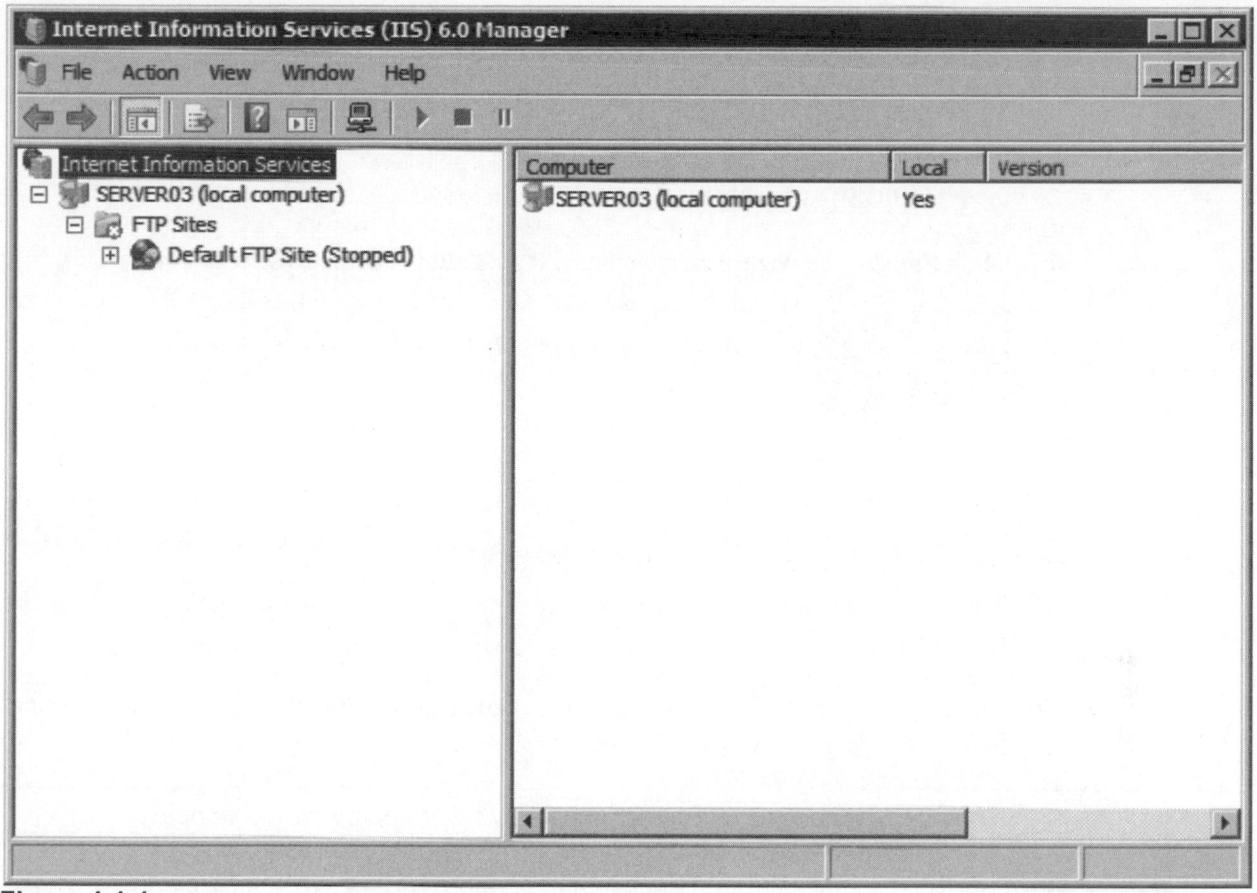

Figure 4-1-1
Internet Information Services (IIS) 6.0 Manager console

10. Right-click the FTP Sites folder and, from the context menu, select New > FTP Site. The FTP Site Creation Wizard appears.

11. Click Next to bypass the *Welcome* page. The *FTP Site Description* page appears.

12. In the description text box, key **FTP6-##,** where ## is the number assigned to your computer. Then click Next. The *IP Address And Port Settings* page appears.

13. Click Next to accept the default settings. The *FTP User Isolation* page appears.

Question 1	Why can an FTP site co-exist with the Default Web Site already installed on the server if neither one is using a unique host name?

14. Leave the Do Not Isolate Users option selected, and click Next. The *FTP Site Home Directory* page appears.

15. In the Path text box, key **C:\Users\Student##**, where ## is the number assigned to your computer, and click Next. The *FTP Site Access Permissions* page appears.

16. Select the Read and Write checkboxes, and click Next. A page appears, stating that the FTP Site Creation Wizard did not complete successfully.

17. Click Finish. The wizard creates the FTP site, but is unable to start it.

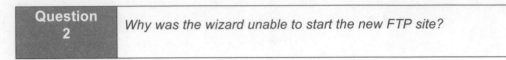

Question 2	Why was the wizard unable to start the new FTP site?

18. Right-click Default FTP Site and, from the context menu, select Start. The site is started.

19. Right-click Default FTP Site again and, from the context menu, select Stop. The site is stopped.

20. Right-click the FTP6-## site you just created and, from the context menu, select Start. The site starts.

> *In a newly installed FTP6 server, the default FTP appears to be stopped, but is not actually in a fully stopped state. Therefore, you must start it and stop it again before you can start the new FTP6-## site you created.*

21. Click Start, and then click All Programs > Accessories > Command Prompt. A command-prompt window appears.

22. In the command-prompt window, key **ftp NT2670Srv##A.contoso##.com**, where ## is the number assigned to your server, and press Enter.

23. When the User prompt appears, key **anonymous**, and press Enter.

24. When the Password prompt appears, press Enter.

Question 3	What happens?

25. Key **quit**, and press Enter.

26. Close the command-prompt window.

27. Open an Internet Explorer window, key **ftp://NT2670Srv##A.contoso##.com**, where ## is the number assigned to your server, and press Enter. An Internet Explorer dialog box appears, prompting you for logon credentials.

28. In the User Name text box, key **contoso##\student##,** where ## is the number assigned to your server.

29. In the Password text box, key **P@ssw0rd**. Then click Log On.

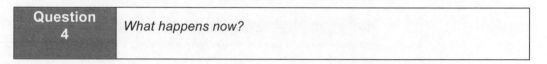

Question 4	What happens now?

30. Press Ctrl+Prt Scr to take a screen shot of the Internet Explorer window. Press Ctrl+V to paste the image on the page provided in the lab4_1_worksheet file.

31. Leave the computer logged on for the next exercise.

Exercise 4-1-3   Configuring FTP6 Security

Overview	In this exercise, configure the security properties available to FTP6 sites.
Completion time	10 minutes

1. In the Internet Information Services (IIS) 6.0 Manager console, right-click the FTP6-## site you created in Exercise 4.2 and, on the context menu, select Properties. The FTP6-## Properties sheet appears, like the sample shown in Figure 4-1-2.

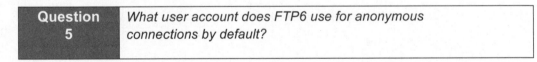

Figure 4-1-2
FTP6-03 Properties sheet

2. Click the Security Accounts tab.

Question 5	*What user account does FTP6 use for anonymous connections by default?*

3. Leave the Allow Anonymous Connections checkbox selected and, in the User Name text box, key **contoso##\Student##,** where ## is the number assigned to your computer.

4. In the Password text box, key **P@ssw0rd**, and click Apply. A Confirm Password dialog box appears.

5. Re-enter the password for confirmation, and click OK.

6. Press Ctrl+Prt Scr to take a screen shot of the Security Accounts tab of the Properties sheet. Press Ctrl+V to paste the image on the page provided in the lab4_1_worksheet file.

7. Click the Home Directory tab.

8. Clear the Write checkbox.

9. Click the Directory Security tab.

10. Select the Denied Access option, and then click Add. The Grant Access dialog box appears.

11. Select the Group Of Computers option.

12. In the IP Address text box, key **172.16.##.0**

13. In the Subnet Mask text box, key **255.255.255.0**.

14. Press Ctrl+Prt Scr to take a screen shot of the Directory Security tab of the Properties sheet. Press Ctrl+V to paste the image on the page provided in the lab4_1_worksheet file.

15. Click OK twice to close the Grant Access dialog box and the Properties sheet.

16. On the NT2670Srv##B computer, log on using your *Administrator* account and the password *P@ssw0rd*. If the Initial Configuration screen appears, close it and also close Server Manager if it appears. Open a command-prompt window, and try to connect to your computer by keying **ftp NT2670Srv##A.contoso##.com**, where ## is the number assigned to your computer.

17. When the User prompt appears, key **anonymous,** and press Enter.

18. When the Password prompt appears, press Enter.

Question 6	*What is the result?*

19. Close all open windows, and log off both computers.

LAB REVIEW QUESTIONS

| Completion time | 5 minutes |

1. In Exercise 4-1-3, after you configure the FTP6 security options, why is it unnecessary for you to log on to connect to the FTP site on your server?

LAB CHALLENGE: CREATING A COMBINED WEB/FTP SITE

| Completion time | 20 minutes |

Your supervisor wants you to create a combined Web/FTP solution that enables a specific user to access his or her user profile folder on your server. To complete this challenge, create a site that provides both HTTP and FTP access to your Student## account's user profile folder (C:\Users\Student##), subject to the following restrictions:

- The HTTP and FTP sites must be accessible using the URLs

  http://student##.contoso##.com and ftp://student##.contoso##.com,

  respectively.

- HTTP access must use Windows Authentication.

- FTP access must use Basic Authentication.

- The site must be accessible only by the Student## user.

- The user must be able to see a directory listing, whether connected using

  HTTP or FTP.

List the tasks you must complete to create and configure the site, and then take two screen shots of the Internet Explorer window showing the HTTP and FTP connections. Paste the image on the page provided in the lab4_1_worksheet file.

LAB 5-1 70-643
USING NETWORK APPLICATION SERVICES

This lab contains the following exercises:

Exercise 5-1-1 Installing Windows Media Services
Exercise 5-1-2 Creating a Publishing Point
Exercise 5-1-3 Creating an Announcement File
Exercise 5-1-4 Establishing a Windows Media Services Connection
Lab Review: Questions
Lab Challenge: Deploying Windows SharePoint Services
Workstation Reset: Return to Baseline

Estimated lab time: 95 minutes

BEFORE YOU BEGIN

The classroom network consists of Windows Server 2008 student server A and B a connected to via an internal local area network. NT2670Srv##A the domain controller for the contoso##.com domain, is running Windows Server 2008. Throughout the labs in this manual, you will install, configure, maintain, and troubleshoot application roles, features, and services on the NT2670Srv##A.

To accommodate various types of classroom arrangements, each lab in this manual assumes that the student servers are in their baseline configuration, as described in Lab 1-2 "Preparing an Application Server." If you have not done so already, complete the initial configuration tasks in Lab 1-2-1, before beginning this lab.

Your instructor should have supplied the information needed to complete the following table:

Student computer name (NT2670Srv##)	
Student account name (Student##)	

Working with Lab Worksheets

Each lab in this manual requires that you answer questions, save images of your screen, or perform other activities that you document in a worksheet named for the lab and task, such as *lab5_1_worksheet*. Your instructor provided you with lab worksheets. As you perform the tasks and exercises in each lab, open the appropriate worksheet file using WordPad, fill in the required information, and save the file to your computer's Student##\Documents folder. Print a copy for your instructor.

The procedure for opening and saving a worksheet file is as follows:

1. Open worksheet document opens in WordPad.

2. Complete all of the exercises in the worksheet.

3. In WordPad, choose Save As from the File menu. The Save As dialog box appears.

4. In the File Name text box, key **lab##_ worksheet_*yourname*** (where lab##_*task*## contains the number of the lab and task you're completing, and *yourname* is your last name), and click Save.

5. Print a copy for your instructor.

SCENARIO

You are a new administrator for Contoso##, Ltd., working on a test deployment of the application server technologies included with Windows Server 2008. In this lab, you explore some of the add-on network applications that Microsoft provides for Windows Server 2008.

After completing this lab, you will be able to:

- Install and configure the Streaming Media Services role
- Install, configure, and use Windows SharePoint Services

Exercise 5-1-1   Installing Windows Media Services

Overview	Windows Server 2008 does not ship with the Streaming Media Services role; it is a separate download. In this exercise, install the Windows Media Services software, which makes the Streaming Media Services role appear in Server Manager.
Completion time	10 minutes

1. Turn on your NT2670Srv##A computer, when the logon screen appears, log on using your *Administrator* account and the password *P@ssw0rd*. If the Initial Configuration screen appears, close it.

2. Your instructor will provide you with the Windows6.0-KB934518-x86-Server.msu for the installation of Windows Media Services software.

3. Double-click the Windows6.0-KB934518-x86-Server.msu file. The Windows Update Standalone Installer message box appears, confirming that you want to install the update.

4. Click OK. The Read These License Terms window appears.

5. Click I Accept to agree to the terms. The *Download And Install Updates* page appears.

6. When the *Installation Complete* page appears, click Close.

7. Open Server Manager, and start the Add Roles Wizard.

Question 1	What change in Server Manager was caused by the Windows Media Services installation you just performed?

8. On the *Select Server Roles* page, select Streaming Media Services, and click Next.

9. Click Next again to bypass the introductory page. The *Select Role Services* page appears, as shown in Figure 5-1-1.

Figure 5-1-1
Select Role Services page in the Add Role Services Wizard

10. Select Web-Based Administration. An Add Role Services And Features Required For Web-Based Administration dialog box appears.

11. Click Add Required Role Services, and then click Next. The *Select Data Transfer Protocols* page appears.

Question 2	*Why is the Hypertext Transfer Protocol (HTTP) option unavailable (gray) in the Select Data Transfer Protocols page?*

12. Click Next to accept the default settings. The *Web Server (IIS)* introductory page appears.

13. Click Next twice to accept the default Web Server (IIS) settings. The *Confirm Installation Selections* page appears.

14. Click Install. The wizard installs the role, and the *Installation Results* page appears.

15. Press Ctrl+Prt Scr to take a screen shot of the *Installation Results* page. Press Ctrl+V to paste the image on the page provided in the lab5_1_worksheet file.

16. Click Close.

17. Leave the computer logged on for the next exercise.

Exercise 5-1-2	Creating a Publishing Point
Overview	In this exercise, create a new publishing point that you can use to deploy multimedia content to network clients on your Windows Media Services server.
Completion time	10 minutes

1. Click Start, and then click Administrative Tools > Windows Media Services. The Windows Media Services console appears, as shown in Figure 5-1-2.

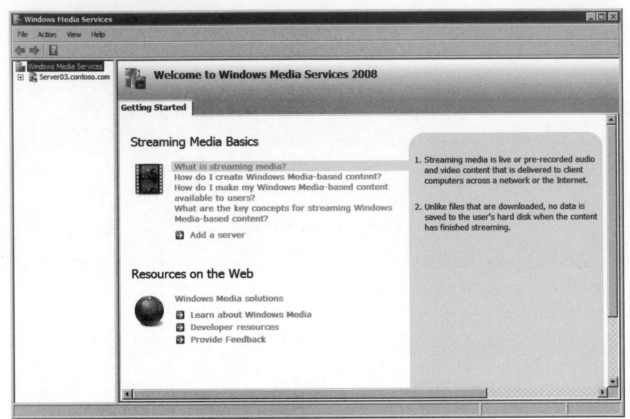

Figure 5-1-2
Windows Media Services console

2. In the scope (left) pane, expand your server, and select the Publishing Points node. The *Publishing Points On NT2670Srv##A.contoso##.com* page appears.

3. Right-click the Publishing Points node and, from the context menu, select Add Publishing Point (Wizard). The Add Publishing Point Wizard appears.

4. Click Next to bypass the *Welcome* page. The *Publishing Point Name* page appears.

5. In the Name text box, key **Stream##**, where ## is the number assigned to your computer, and click Next. The *Content Type* page appears.

6. Select the One File option, and click Next. The *Publishing Point Type* page appears.

7. Select the On-Demand Publishing Point option, and click Next. The *Existing Publishing Point* page appears.

8. Leave the Add A New Publishing Point option selected, and click Next. The *File Location* page appears.

9. Click Browse. The Windows Media Browse dialog box appears.

10. Select the Industrial.wmv media file, and click Select File.

11. On the *File Location* page, click Next. The *Unicast Logging* page appears.

12. Select the Yes, Enable Logging For This Publishing Point checkbox, and click Next. The *Publishing Point Summary* page appears.

13. Click Next. The *Completing The Add Publishing Point Wizard* page appears.

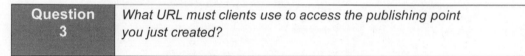

Question 3	What URL must clients use to access the publishing point you just created?

14. Clear the After The Wizard Finishes checkbox, and click Finish. The new publishing point appears on the *Publishing Points On NT2670Srv##A.contoso##.com* page.

15. Press Ctrl+Prt Scr to take a screen shot of the *Publishing Points On NT2670Srv##A.contoso##.com* page. Press Ctrl+V to paste the image on the page provided in the lab5_1_worksheet file.

16. Leave the computer logged on for the next exercise.

Exercise 5-1-3   Creating an Announcement File

Overview	In this exercise, create an announcement file and a Web page that clients can use to access multimedia content on the publishing point you created in Exercise 5-1-2.
Completion time	5 minutes

1. In the Windows Media Services console, expand the Publishing Points node, and select the Stream## publishing point you just created, as shown in Figure 5-1-3.

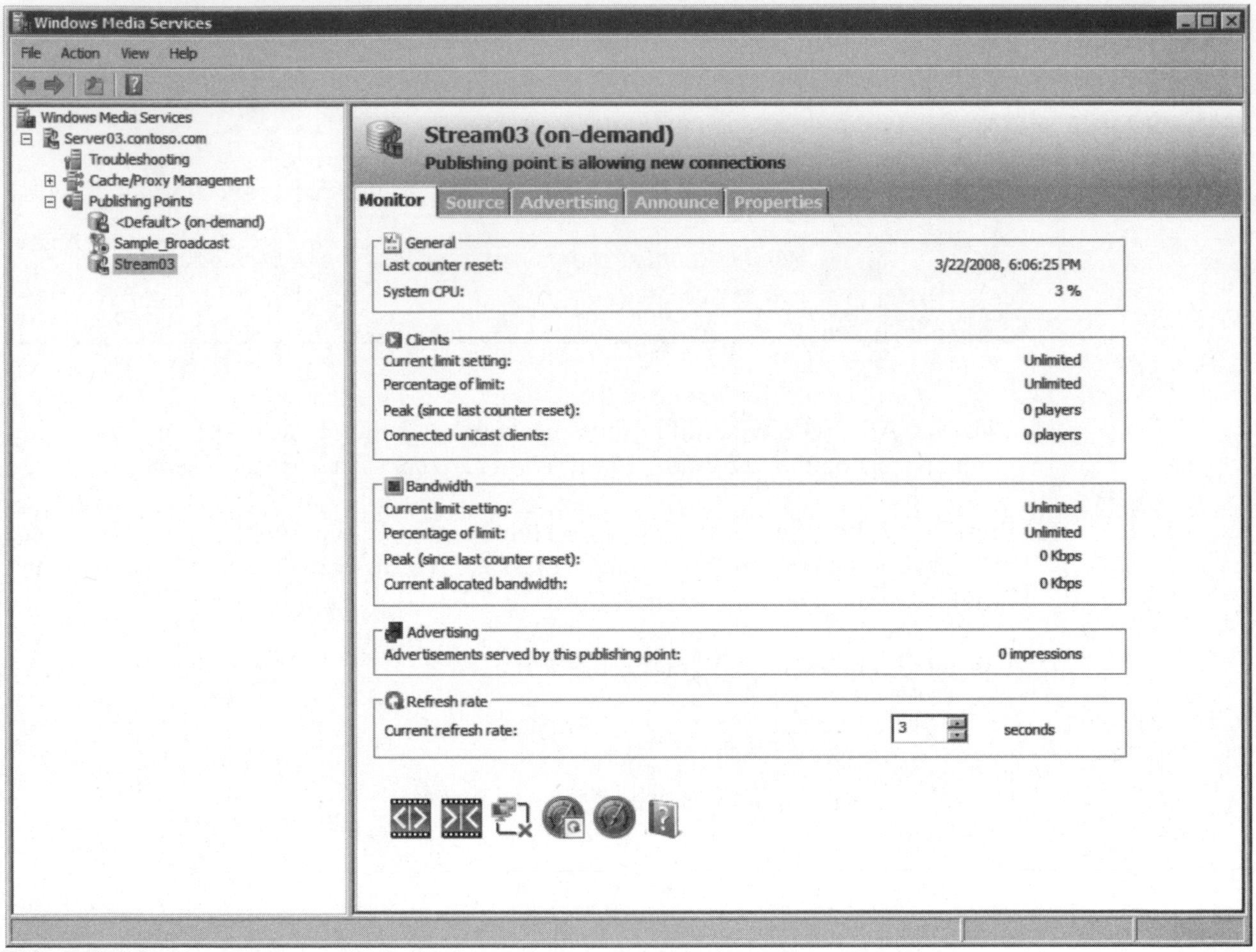

Figure 5-1-3
Monitor tab of a Windows Media Services publishing point

2. In the detail pane, click the Announce tab.

3. Click the Run Unicast Announcement Wizard button. The *Welcome To The Unicast Announcement Wizard* page appears.

4. Click Next. The *Access The Content* page appears.

5. Click Next to accept the default URL. The *Save Announcement Options* page appears.

6. Select the Create A Web Page With An Embedded Player And A Link To The Content checkbox.

7. Press Ctrl+Prt Scr to take a screen shot of the *Save Announcement Options* page. Press Ctrl+V to paste the image on the page provided in the lab5_1_worksheet file.

8. Click Next. The *Edit Announcement Metadata* page appears.

9. Click Next to accept the default values. The *Completing The Unicast Announcement Wizard* page appears.

10. Clear the Test Files When This Wizard Finishes checkbox, and click Finish. The wizard creates the announcement file and a Web page containing the embedded player.

	Does the announcement file the wizard created contain the actual multimedia content? How can you tell?

11. Leave the computer logged on for the next exercise.

Exercise 5-1-4	Establishing a Windows Media Services Connection
Overview	In this exercise, test your Windows Media Services server by using the Web page you created to access your new publishing point.
Completion time	10 minutes

1. Open Internet Explorer. In the address box, key **https://NT2670Srv##A.contoso##.com/stream##.htm**, and then press Enter. The *Announcement For Publishing Point Stream##* page appears, as shown in Figure 5-1-4.

> **NOTE**
> *If an information bar appears in the Internet Explorer window warning you about the potential dangers of ActiveX content, click the bar and allow IE to run the ActiveX control.*

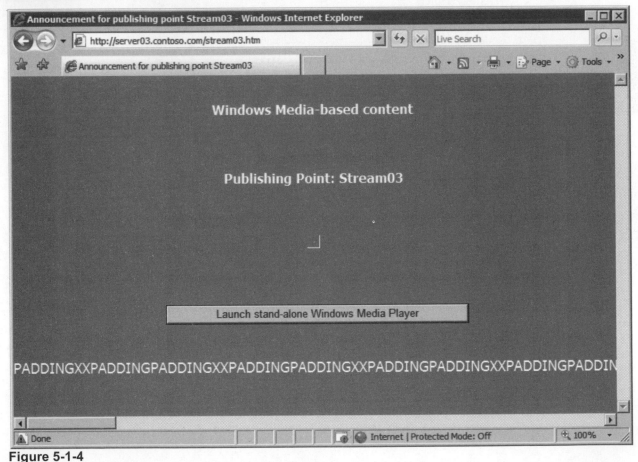

Figure 5-1-4
Announcement For Publishing Point Stream## page

Question 5	*What happens after the Announcement For Publishing Point Stream## page appears?*

2. Click the Launch Stand-Alone Windows Media Player button.

Question 6	*What happens?*

3. Open the Server Manager console, and start the Add Features Wizard.

4. On the *Select Features* page, select the Desktop Experience feature, and click Next.

5. Click Install. The wizard installs the selected feature.

6. Click Close, and restart the computer.

7. After the computer starts, Server Manager reloads itself and completes the feature installation.

8. Click Close.

9. Open Internet Explorer and try again to connect to the URL http://NT2670Srv##A.contoso##.com/stream##.htm.

Question 7	*What is the result?*

10. Press Ctrl+Prt Scr to take a screen shot of the *Announcement For Publishing Point Stream##* page showing the embedded multimedia content. Press Ctrl+V to paste the image on the page provided in the lab5_1_worksheet file.

11. Close all open windows, and log off of your computer.

LAB REVIEW QUESTIONS

Completion time	5 minutes

1. When a client computer accesses multimedia content by executing an announcement file on a media server, should Windows Media Player be installed on the client or the server?

2. In its default state, immediately after installation, is Windows Media Services ready to stream multimedia content to clients? Why or why not?

3. In Exercise 5-1-4, why does the multimedia file not play the first time you access the *Announcement For Publishing Point Stream##* page in Internet Explorer?

LAB CHALLENGE: DEPLOYING WINDOWS SHAREPOINT SERVICES

Completion time	40 minutes

The director of the IT department is considering a large deployment of Windows SharePoint Services to enable network users to share documents and collaborate on projects at the workgroup and departmental levels. To help her decide, she wants you to deploy Windows SharePoint Services on a Windows Server 2008 test server by completing each of the following tasks:

- Install and configure Windows SharePoint Services.

- Add the Students group as SharePoint team site users, giving them the Contribute permission.

- Add a new shared document to the Team Site library.

- Add a calendar entry scheduling a staff meeting.

> **NOTE**
>
> *Windows SharePoint Services is not supplied with Windows Server 2008. It is available as a free download from Microsoft's Web site. However, your instructor placed the software on the network server in the \\ServerDC\Install\SharePoint folder.*

List the steps you must perform to complete these tasks, and take screen shots demonstrating that you have completed each task. Paste the images on the page provided in the lab5_1_worksheet file.

WORKSTATION RESET: RETURN TO BASELINE

Completion time	15 minutes

After this lab, you will not need the Windows Media Services role or the Windows SharePoint Services application. To return the computer to its baseline state, complete the following procedures.

1. On your NT2670Srv##A and NT2670Srv##B computers open the Server Manager console, and remove all of the roles you installed during this lab. Restart the computer.

2. Open the Programs And Features control panel, and uninstall Microsoft Windows SharePoint Services 3.0. Restart the computer.

PART 2

Customized Excerpts from

Microsoft® Official Academic Course

Microsoft® Exchange Server® 2007 Configuration

Microsoft Certified Technology Specialist Exam 70-236 Lab Manual

LAB 6-1 70-236

DNS RESOLUTION AND ACTIVE DIRECTORY OBJECTS

This lab contains the following exercises:

Exercise 6-1-1 Configuring Your Lab Computers
Exercise 6-1-2 Creating and Managing Active Directory Objects
Lab Review: Questions

Estimated lab time: 90 minutes

BEFORE YOU BEGIN

Lab 6-1 assumes that setup has been completed as specified in the setup document and that your workstation has connectivity to your internal network and the other virtual lab computers on your host.

SCENARIO

You are the network administrator for your organization. Before implementing Active Directory and Exchange Server 2007 within your organization, you wish to investigate how DNS and Active Directory Objects function as well as explore the structure and features within Exchange Server 2007.

After completing this lab, you will be able to:

- Understand DNS configuration
- Understand Exchange Server 2007 structure and features

Exercise 6-1-1   Configuring Your Lab Computers

Overview	Before performing the exercises in this lab manual, you must ensure that the two instances of Windows Server 2008 are configured according to the information that you supply in Figure 6-1-2. To complete this lab exercise, NT2670Srv##A and NT2670Srv##B must be started.
Completion time	20 minutes

To perform the exercises in this lab manual, you will need to have two full instances of Windows Server 2008 Standard 32 bit Edition installed as virtual appliances using VMware. This will allow you to interface with both instances of Windows Server 2008 from the same computer during the exercises. Confirm that the Virtual Machine settings for the Network adapter are set to "Host only."

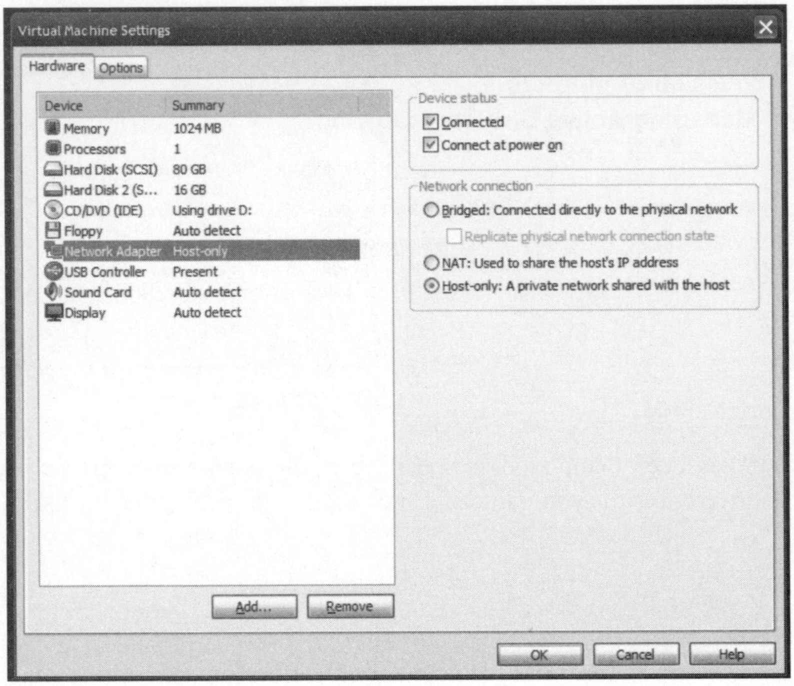

Figure 6-1-1 Virtual Machine Settings

For simplicity, the Administrator account on each instance of Windows Server 2008 should have the same password (P@ssw0rd). In addition, each instance of Windows Server 2008 will have a different computer name: NT2670Srv##A and NT2670Srv##B, where ## is a unique number assigned to you by your instructor. Each instance of Windows Server 2008 will need to have a single network interface configured with a unique IP address as well as a subnet mask and default gateway. The DNS server configured within the network interfaces on NT2670Srv##B should be the IP address of NT2670Srv##A. The IP address for NT2670Srv##B should be one more than that of NT2670Srv##A, (i.e. 172.16.##.2)

Next, fill in the appropriate name and IP configuration for your computer in Figure 6-1-2 using the space provided. You can use this information for future reference.

	Windows Server 2008	Windows Server 2008
	NT2670Srv##A	NT2670Srv##B
IP Address		
Subnet Mask		
Default Gateway		
DNS Server		

Figure 6-1-2 Your computer and virtual machine configuration

NOTE	*In this lab, you will see the characters ##. When you see these characters, substitute the two-digit number assigned to your computer.*

Exercise 6-1-2   Creating and Managing Active Directory Objects

Overview	In this exercise, you will create new OU, user, group, and computer objects. In addition, you will disable and reset user accounts as well as add user accounts to groups. Moreover, you will disable and reset a computer account.
	To complete this lab exercise, NT2670Srv##A and NT2670Srv##B must be started and have network access.
Completion time	60 minutes

1. Turn on your NT2670Srv##A and NT2670Srv##B computers. On the NT2670Srv##A computer, when the logon screen appears, log on using your *Administrator* account and the password *P@ssw0rd*. If the Initial Configuration screen appears, close it.

2. Click Start, Administrative Tools, and Active Directory Users and Computers. The Active Directory Users and Computers console appears.

3. In the left pane, right click Contoso##.com and select New followed by Organizational Unit from the menu.

4. At the New Object—Organizational Unit window type **Accounting** and click OK.

5. Use the procedure detailed in the previous two steps to create the **Marketing**, **Sales**, and **Production** organizational units (OUs) under your domain.

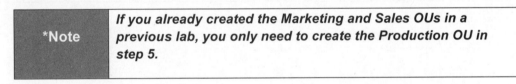

*Note	*If you already created the Marketing and Sales OUs in a previous lab, you only need to create the Production OU in step 5.*

6. In the left pane, right click the Sales OU object and select New followed by User from the menu.

7. At the New Object—User window, type **Sophia** in the First name dialog box, **Boren** in the Last name dialog box, **sophia.boren** in the User logon name dialog box and click Next.

8. Type the password **P@ssw0rd** in both password dialog boxes. Next, deselect **User must change password at next logon** and select **User cannot change password** and **Password never expires**.

9. Click Next. Click Finish to create the user account.

10. In the right pane, right click the Sophia Boren user account and select Properties. Highlight the Organization tab, type **Sales** in the Department dialog box, and click OK.

11. Use the procedure detailed in Steps 6 to 10, create the other user accounts listed in Table 6-1-1 in the appropriate OUs with the appropriate Department attributes. Each user should have a logon name of **firstname.lastname** (lowercase).

Table 6-1-1
User account information

User Name	OU/Department
Sophia Boren	Sales
Mel Booker	Accounting
Celine DeVries	Accounting
Mike Moritz	Marketing
Mark Daly	Production
Tiger Smith	Accounting
Mog Roombas	Sales
Jacques Guillere	Sales
Juan Ton	Marketing
Sarah Parkers	Production
Lois Lipshitz	Production
Jessica Augustus	Accounting
Tom Hurt	Production
Bernadette Jones	Production
Jennifer Coupland	Production
Courtney Davies	Marketing
Lisa Lackner	Sales
Mathew Kropf	Production
Matt Adams	Sales
David Schwan	Production

12. In the left pane, right click Contoso##.com and select New followed by Group from the menu.

13. At the New Object—Group window type **Managers** in the Group name dialog box and ensure that Global is selected in the Group scope section and Security is selected in the Group Type section. Click OK when finished.

14. Use the procedure detailed in the previous two steps to create the **Executives** and **Supervisors** groups under your domain.

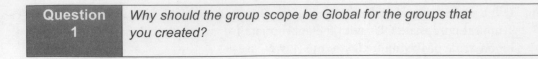

15. In the left pane, highlight the Sales OU. Next, right click the Sophia Boren user account in the right pane and select Properties. Highlight the Member of tab of the user's properties.

16. Click the Add button. In the Select Groups window click Advanced, and then click Find Now button. Select the Managers group and click OK to return to the Select Groups window.

17. Click OK to return to the user's properties window.

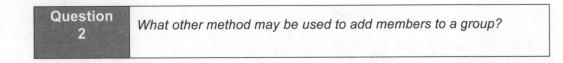

18. Use the procedure detailed in the previous three steps to assign the appropriate users to the correct groups as described in Table 6-1-2.

Table 6-1-2
User group information

User Name	Group
Sophia Boren	Managers
Mel Booker	Supervisors
Celine DeVries	Executives
Mike Moritz	Managers
Mark Daly	Supervisors
Tiger Smith	Managers
Meg Roombas	Supervisors
Jacques Guillere	Executives
Juan Ton	Managers
Sarah Parkers	Supervisors
Lois Lipshitz	Supervisors
Jessica Augustus	Executives
Tom Hurt	Managers
Bernadette Jones	Managers
Jennifer Coupland	Supervisors
Courtney Davies	Executives
Lisa Lackner	Managers
Mathew Kropf	Supervisors
Matt Adams	Executives
David Schwan	Supervisors

19. In the left pane, highlight the Production OU. Next, right click the Lois Lipshitz user account in the right pane and select Disable Account. Click OK at the confirmation window.

20. In the left pane, highlight the Accounting OU. Next, right click the Tiger Smith user account in the right pane and select Reset Password. Type **Secret123** in both password dialog boxes and click OK.

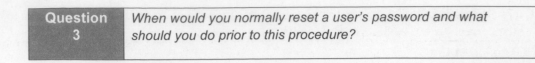

Question 3	When would you normally reset a user's password and what should you do prior to this procedure?

21. In the left pane, right click the Accounting OU and select New followed by Computer from the menu.

22. At the New Object—Computer window type **Client1** in the Computer name dialog box. Ensure that Domain Admins will be allowed to join the computer with the NetBIOS name Client1 to the domain and click OK to create the computer account.

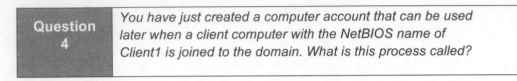

Question 4	You have just created a computer account that can be used later when a client computer with the NetBIOS name of Client1 is joined to the domain. What is this process called?

23. Right click the Client1 computer account and select Reset Account. Click Yes to confirm the reset operation.

Question 5	When would you normally reset a computer account?
Question 6	What must you do on the client computer after resetting a computer account?

24. Right click the Client1 computer account and select Disable Account. Click Yes to confirm the reset operation and click OK to close the confirmation window.

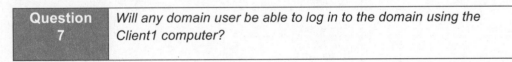

Question 7	Will any domain user be able to log in to the domain using the Client1 computer?

25. Close the Active Directory Users and Computers console, and log off both computers.

LAB REVIEW QUESTIONS

Completion time   10 minutes

1. Describe what you learned by completing this lab.

2. How does the DNS round-robin feature load balance connections when there are more than one MX or associated A record to describe email servers for a domain?

3. In Exercise 6-1-2, you configured the same password for each user account. Is this a good practice? Explain.

LAB 6-2   70-236
CONFIGURING A WINDOWS 7 CLIENT MACHINE AND INSTALLING MICROSOFT OUTLOOK

This lab contains the following exercises:

Exercise 6-2-1 Performing Initial Virtual Server Image
Exercise 6-2-2 Exploring Windows 7
Exercise 6-2-3 Joining a Windows 7 Machine to the Active Directory Domain

Estimated lab time: 90 minutes

Exercise 6-2-1	Performing Initial Virtual Server Image
Overview	You are creating a new computer virtual appliance with Windows 7 Professional using VMware Player. Your first task is to create a new Virtual Machine and install Windows 7 Professional 32bit with appropriate settings for the test lab network.
Completion time	30 minutes

1.   Start VMWare Player and create a new Virtual Machine. Make sure that you have your Windows 7 Professional 32-bit installation disk in the DVD player.

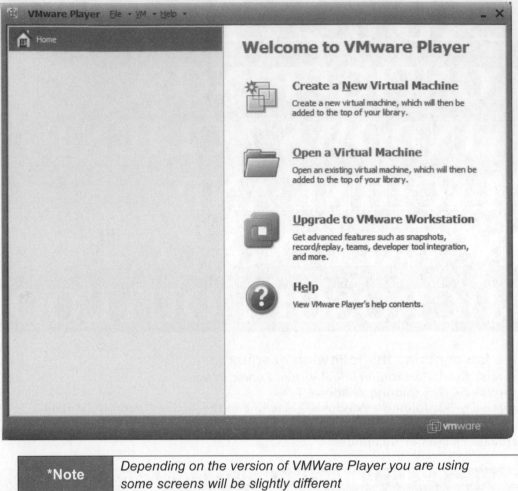

*Note	Depending on the version of VMWare Player you are using some screens will be slightly different

2.   Select the installation disk and click next.

New Virtual Machine Wizard   ✕

Welcome to the New Virtual Machine Wizard
A virtual machine is like a physical computer; it needs an operating system. How will you install the guest operating system?

Install from:

◉ Installer disc:

> GRMCPRFRER_EN_DVD (D:)   ▼

ⓘ Windows 7 detected.
This operating system will use Easy Install. (What's this?)

○ Installer disc image file (iso):

[   ] ▼   Browse...

○ I will install the operating system later.

The virtual machine will be created with a blank hard disk.

[Help]   [< Back] [Next >] [Cancel]

*Note	If you are using a Windows 7 Professional .iso, Select Installer disc image file (iso): and browse to the location of the .iso file.

3. Skip the Product key and use "Student ## "where ## is the number provided by your instructor as the full name, and P@ssw0rd as password.

New Virtual Machine Wizard

Easy Install Information
This is used to install Windows 7.

Windows product key

[- - - -]

Personalize Windows

Full name: Student99

Password: ••••••••   (optional)

Confirm: ••••••••

[Help]   [< Back] [Next >]   [Cancel]

New Virtual Machine Wizard

Easy Install Information
This is used to install Windows 7.

Windows product key

[| - - - -]

Version of Windows to install

[Windows 7 Home Basic   ▼]

Personalize Windows

Full name: George

Password: [   ]   (optional)

Confirm: [   ]

☐ Log on automatically (requires a password)

[Help]   [< Back] [Next >]   [Cancel]

*Note	*Depending on the version of VMWare Player you are using you may need to choose Windows 7 Professional as the Operating System to install during this step. Please ensure Windows 7 Professional is the version chosen.*

*Note	*Online students can use Student01 as the name of their student account.*

4. You would like to continue. Click Yes.

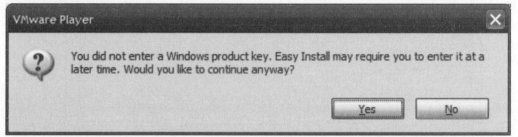

5. Name your server Workstation## where ## is the number assigned by your instructor. And store the new Appliance in a newly created Windows 7 folder in you're my Virtual Machines folder on your removable USB hard disk.

*Note	*Online students can use Workstation01 as their Virtual Machine Name.*

6. Click next and choose the default disk size of 40GB, and click next.

New Virtual Machine Wizard

Specify Disk Capacity
How large do you want this disk to be?

The virtual machine's hard disk is stored as one or more files on the host computer's physical disk. These file(s) start small and become larger as you add applications, files, and data to your virtual machine.

Maximum disk size (GB):   40.0

Recommended size for Windows 7: 40 GB

⊙ Store virtual disk as a single file

◯ Split virtual disk into 2 GB files

Splitting the disk makes it easier to move the virtual machine to another computer.

Help   < Back   Next >   Cancel

7. Remember to customize Hardware and select Advance and "legacy emulation" for the CD/DVD drive. Also change the Network Adapter Settings to Host Only.

New Virtual Machine Wizard

Ready to Create Virtual Machine
Click Finish to create the virtual machine and start installing Windows 7 and then VMware Tools.

The virtual machine will be created with the following settings:

Name:	Workstation99
Location:	E:\My Virtual Machines\Windows 7
Version:	Workstation 6.5-7.0
Operating System:	Windows 7
Hard Disk:	40 GB
Memory:	1024 MB
Network Adapter:	Bridged
Other Devices:	CD/DVD, Floppy, USB Controller, Sound Card

Customize Hardware...

☑ Power on this virtual machine after creation

< Back   Finish   Cancel

Advanced

Virtual device node

○ SCSI:

SCSI 0:0 (Reserved)

◉ IDE:

IDE 1:0 New CD/DVD (IDE)

Troubleshooting

☑ Legacy emulation

OK   Cancel   Help

Hardware

Device	Summary
Memory	1024 MB
Processors	1
New CD/DVD (...	Using drive D:
Floppy	Auto detect
Network Adapter	Bridged
USB Controller	Present
Sound Card	Auto detect
Display	Auto detect

Memory

Specify the amount of memory allocated to this virtual machine. The memory size must be a multiple of 4 MB.

Memory for this virtual machine:

1024 ▲▼ MB

4   2995

△ Guest OS recommended minimum: 1024 MB

△ Recommended memory: 1024 MB

▲ Maximum recommended memory: 2892 MB

(Memory swapping may occur beyond this size.)

Maximum configurable memory: 32768 MB

Add...   Remove

OK   Cancel   Help

8. Click finish and install Windows 7 Professional 32-bit. Remember uncheck the automatic activation and do not enter a key.

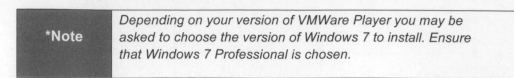

> ***Note**   *Depending on your version of VMWare Player you may be asked to choose the version of Windows 7 to install. Ensure that Windows 7 Professional is chosen.*

9. After you have finished the installation of your Windows 7 Professional workstation and shut it down. Create a second folder in the Windows 7 folder and copy the contents of your first server folder to this new folder, giving you a second virtual appliance and a baseline backup.

E:\My Virtual Machines

File   Edit   View   Favorites   Tools   Help

Back • ⊙ • 🗁 🔎 Search 📂 Folders 🗇 🗇 ✕ 🕘 ▦▾

Address 🗁 E:\My Virtual Machines   ✔ ➡ Go

Name ▲	Size	Type	Date Modified	Attributes
🗀 Windows 7		File Folder	5/10/2011 11:50 AM	
🗀 Windows 7 Backup		File Folder	5/10/2011 11:53 AM	

2 objects   0 bytes   💻 My Computer

Exercise 6-2-2	Exploring Windows 7
Overview	In order to familiarize yourself with the new Operating System being rolled out in your organization, you decide to manipulate some common features to see how they differ from previous Windows versions. In this exercise you will work with screen saver and other display properties.
Completion time	30 minutes

1. Turn on the Workstation## computer and log on using your Student## account and the password P@ssw0rd.
2. Right Click on Computer and Select Properties (you can also use Windows Key + Pause). The Computers Property sheet appears.

3. Click the Change Settings Button. The System Properties Dialog Box appears.
4. Click Change. The Computer Name/Domain Name Changes Dialog Box appears.

5. Enter Workstation## in the Computer Name Text Box.

Computer Name/Domain Changes

You can change the name and the membership of this computer. Changes might affect access to network resources. More information

Computer name:

Workstation99

Full computer name:

Workstation99

More...

Member of

○ Domain:

● Workgroup:

WORKGROUP

OK   Cancel

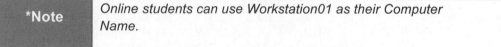*Note	Online students can use Workstation01 as their Computer Name.

6. Click OK to accept the change. You will be prompted to restart the machine Click OK. Click OK on the System Properties screen and choose restart now.

Computer Name/Domain Changes

ⓘ You must restart your computer to apply these changes

Before restarting, save any open files and close all programs.

OK

7. When the computer has completed restarting, log on using your Student## account and the password P@ssw0rd.

8. Right Click on the Desktop and select Screen Resolution. Change it if necessary.

Exercise 6-2-3	Joining a Windows 7 Machine to the Active Directory Domain
Overview	The client computers in the network must now be joined to the domain to reap the full benefits of an Active Directory environment. In this exercise you will join your Windows 7 machine to the Active Directory domain and log in with one of the user accounts created in Exercise 6-2-1.
Completion time	30 minutes

1. Turn on your NT2670Srv##A computer, when the logon screen appears, log on using your *Administrator* account and the password *P@ssw0rd*. If the Initial Configuration screen appears, close it.

2. On the Workstation## computer, click Start and then click Control Panel. The Control Panel window appears.

3. Click Network and Internet > Network and Sharing Center. The Network and Sharing Center control panel appears.

4. In the Network and Sharing Center control panel select Change Adapter Settings. The Network Connections window appears.

5. Right-click the Local Area Connection icon and, from the context menu, select Properties. The Local Area Connection Properties sheet appears.

6. Clear the Internet Protocol Version 6 (TCP/IPv6) checkbox.

7. Select Internet Protocol Version 4 (TCP/IPv4) and click Properties. The Internet Protocol Version 4 (TCP/IPv4) Properties sheet appears.

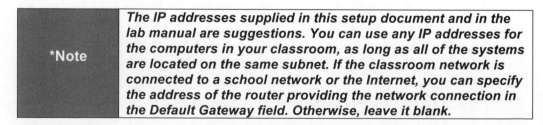

8. Select the Use the following IP address and the Use the following DNS server addresses radio buttons and enter the following information:

- IP Address: 172.16.##.3 (Where ## is the number assigned by your instructor)
- Subnet Mask: 255.255.255.0
- Preferred DNS Server: 172.16.##.1

*Note   The IP addresses supplied in this setup document and in the lab manual are suggestions. You can use any IP addresses for the computers in your classroom, as long as all of the systems are located on the same subnet. If the classroom network is connected to a school network or the Internet, you can specify the address of the router providing the network connection in the Default Gateway field. Otherwise, leave it blank.

9. Click OK twice to close the two Properties sheets. Close the Network Connections window.

10. Right Click on Computer and Select Properties (you can also use Windows Key + Pause). The Computers Property sheet appears.

11. Click the Change Settings Button. The System Properties Dialog Box appears.
12. Click Change. The Computer Name/Domain Name Changes Dialog Box appears.

13. In the Member of section of the Computer Name/Domain Name Changes Dialog Box select the Domain radio button and enter contoso##.com in the Domain text box.

Question 1	*Could you have used your local Student## account to join the contoso##.Local domain? Why or why not?*

14. Click OK to accept the change. A Windows Security dialog box appears. Enter Administrator in the username text box and P@ssw0rd in the password text box and click OK.

*Note	*If you receive a DNS error at this step check the IP address configurations on both machines. If that does not resolve the issue change the VMWare Player network settings on both machines to Bridged.*

15. A message appears welcoming you to the contoso##.com domain. Click OK.

16. You will be prompted to restart the machine Click OK. Click OK on the System Properties screen and choose restart now.

17. When the computer has completed restarting, log on using your Administrator account and the password P@ssw0rd.

*Note	***In order to log in you may have to click switch user and enter contoso##\Administrator as the username.***

18. Right Click on Computer and Select Properties (you can also use Windows Key + Pause). The Computers Property sheet appears.

19. Take a screen shot showing the Computer Properties window displaying that Workstation## is now a member of the contoso##.com domain by pressing Alt+ Prt Scr, and then paste the resulting image into the Lab6_2_worksheet file in the page provided by pressing Ctrl + V.

20. Install Office 2007 with the Outlook 2007 components at minimum from the Office 2007 installation media that you previously received.

21. Close all open windows, and log off of both computers.

LAB 7-1 70-236

DEPLOYING MICROSOFT EXCHANGE SERVER 2007 SP3

This lab contains the following exercises:

Exercise 7-1-1 Deploying the First Exchange Server
Exercise 7-1-2 Deploying the Second Exchange Server
Lab Review: Questions
Lab Challenge: Performing an Unattended Exchange Server Installation

Estimated lab time: 210 minutes

BEFORE YOU BEGIN

Lab 7-1 assumes that setup has been completed as specified in the setup document and that NT2670Srv##A and NT2670Srv##B have connectivity to the classroom network and the Internet. Moreover, Lab 7-1 assumes that you have completed the exercises in previous Labs.

NOTE	*In this lab, you will see the characters ##. When you see these characters, substitute the two-digit number assigned to your computer.*

SCENARIO

You plan to deploy Exchange Server 2007 SP3 Enterprise Edition within your organization. NT2670Srv##A will be the first Exchange server within the organization and host the Mailbox, Hub, CAS, and UM roles. To provide fault tolerance and load balancing for the Mailbox, Hub, and CAS roles in the HeadOffice site, you will also install Exchange Server 2007 on NT2670Srv##B with the Mailbox, Hub, and CAS roles. Figure 7-1-1 depicts the Exchange server roles that will be installed during this lab.

Exchange Server 2007	Exchange Server 2007
NT2670Srv##A	NT2670Srv##B
Mailbox Role	Mailbox Role
Hub Role	Hub Role
CAS Role	CAS Role
UM Role	

HeadOffice Site

Figure 7-1-1
Exchange server roles for NT2670Srv##A and NT2670Srv##B

In the Lab Challenge, you will install the UM role on NT2670Srv##B using an unattended installation.

After completing this lab, you will be able to:

- Prepare a Windows Server 2008 computer for Exchange Server 2007 installation

- Install Exchange Server 2007 in different configurations

- Verify the installation of Exchange server roles

- Perform an unattended Exchange Server 2007 installation

Exchange Server 2007 Prerequisite Notes:

NOTE: Students must install Exchange Server 2007 SP3.

NOTE: Students may need to perform a Windows update before installing Exchange Server 2007 SP3.

NOTE: Students may need to re-install the Desktop Experinace Feature.

NOTE: Students should download Windows installer 4.5 before attempting the intallation of Exchange.

NOTE: Students will need to install PowerShell through the Features console. After the install the students will need to close down Exchange setup and restart the setup. Donot click on Retry, it will not work.

NOTE: Students will need to install IIS 7.

NOTE: Students will need to install Remote Differential compression.

To address this issue, follow the appropriate steps to install the required IIS 7 components on the destination computer, and then run Microsoft Exchange Setup again.

Install the IIS 7 Components for the CAS server role by using the Windows Server 2008 Server Manager.

1. Click **Start**, click **Administrative Tools**, and then click **Server Manager**.

2. In the navigation pane, expand **Roles**, right-click **Web Server (IIS),** and then click **Add Role Services**.

3. In the **Select Role Services** pane, scroll down to **IIS**.

4. In the **Security** area, click to select the following check boxes:

   - **Basic Authentication**
   - **Digest Authentication**
   - **Windows Authentication**

5. In the **Performance** area, click to select the following check boxes:

   - **Static Compression**
   - **Dynamic Compression**

6. In the **Select Role Services** pane, click **Next**, and then click **Install** in the **Confirm Installations Selections** pane.

7. Click **Close** to exit the Add Role Services wizard.

Install the IIS 7 Components for the Mailbox server role by using the Windows Server 2008 Server Manager.

1. Click **Start**, click **Administrative Tools**, and then click **Server Manager**.

2. In the navigation pane, expand **Roles**, right-click **Web Server (IIS),** and then click **Add Role Services**.

3. In the **Select Role Services** pane, scroll down to **IIS**.

4. In the **Security** area, click to select the following check boxes:

    - **Basic Authentication**
    - **Windows Authentication**

5. In the **Select Role Services** pane, click **Next**, and then click **Install** in the **Confirm Installations Selections** pane.

6. Click **Close** to exit the Add Role Services wizard.

> **NOTE**
>
> *In Exercises 7-1-1 and 7-1-2, you will install Exchange Server 2007. Prior to each installation, you will need to install the necessary software prerequisites as well as prepare the Active Directory domain for Exchange Server 2007.*
>
> *You can install the 32-bit or 64-bit version of Exchange Server 2007 SP3 Enterprise Edition in Exercises 7-1-1 and 7-1-2. However, if you wish to install the 64-bit version of Exchange Server 2007, you must have a 64-bit installation of Windows Server 2008.*
>
> *After each installation, you will verify the installation of the server roles, view installation logs, and update Exchange Server 2007 using Microsoft Update. Although you would normally configure Automatic Updates or WSUS to perform continuous updates for your Windows Server 2008 operating system and Exchange Server 2007, this will use unnecessary bandwidth in the classroom. As a result, we will not be performing these actions in this exercise.*
>
> *In a production environment, you would also enter an Exchange Server 2007 license key following installation. However, in Exercises 7-1-1 and 7-1-2, no license key is necessary because we will be using Exchange Server 2007 in evaluation mode throughout this lab manual.*

Exercise 7-1-1	Deploying the First Exchange Server
Overview	In the following exercise, you will install Exchange Server 2007 SP3 Enterprise Edition on NT2670Srv## with the Mailbox, Hub, CAS, and UM roles as depicted earlier in Figure 7-1-1. To complete this lab exercise, NT2670Srv## and NT2670Srv##B must be started and have network access.
Completion time	100 minutes

1. Turn on your NT2670Srv##A and NT2670Srv##B computers. On the NT2670Srv##A computer, when the logon screen appears, log on using your *Administrator* account and the password *P@ssw0rd*. If the Initial Configuration screen appears, close it.

2. Click Start and click My Computer. Navigate to where you copied the Exchange Server 2007 media folder, open it and double click the **setup.exe** file.

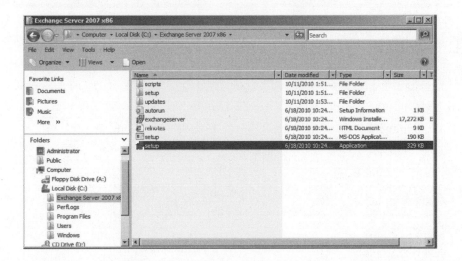

3. The Microsoft Exchange 2007 Setup page appears. Your first step is to install Microsoft Windows PowerShell. Follow the instructions to install PowerShell.

4. Open Server manager from the Start/Administrative Tools icon. In the scope pane, select the Features node, and click Add Features. The Add Features Wizard appears, displaying the *Select Features* page.

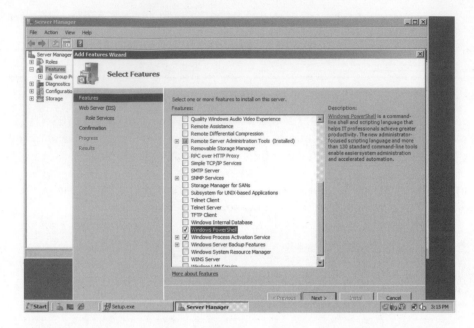

5. Click the Windows PowerShell checkbox and Next, then Install.

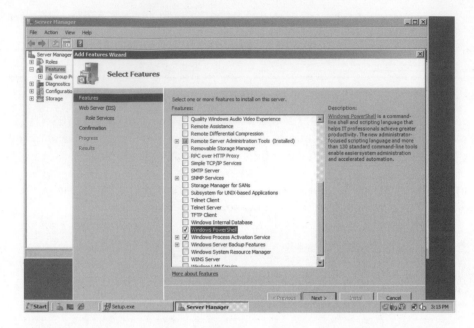

6. Close the Server Manager Window and return to the Exchange Server 2007 Install page.

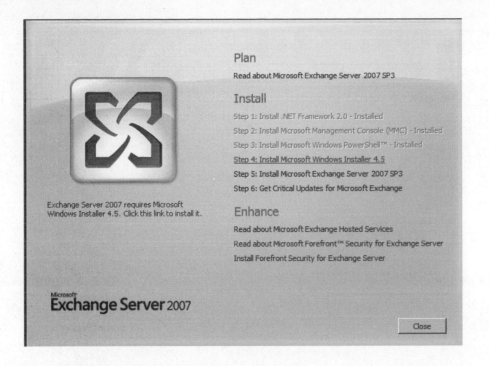

7. At the Exchange Server 2007 welcome screen, You must **Install Windows Installer 4.5** via the Windows6.0-KB942288-v2-x86.msu file found in the Exchange Server 2007 x86 folder you previously copied. After it is installed reboot your computer, log on as administrator and return to the Exchange Server 2007 screen by clicking on the setup icon in the Exchange Server folder.

8. Click **Step 5: Install Microsoft Exchange Server 2007 SP3**. Be Patient as It Takes
    Time!

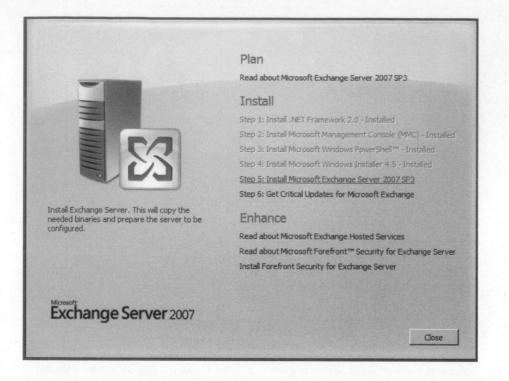

9. At the Exchange Server 2007 SP3 Setup wizard, click Next.

10. At the License Agreement page, select **I accept the terms in the license agreement** and click Next.

11. At the Error Reporting page, ensure that No is selected and click Next.

12. At the Installation Type page, select Custom Exchange Server Installation and click Next.

Question 1	What server roles and components are installed if you select Typical Exchange Server Installation from the Installation Type page?

13. At the Server Role Selection page, select **Mailbox Role**, **Client Access Role**, **Hub Transport Role**, **Unified Messaging Server Role**, and **Management Tools** *(Selected by Default)*. Click Next.

14. At the Exchange Organization page enter Contoso## and click Next.

15. At the Client Settings page, select Yes to allow Entourage and Outlook 2003 and earlier MAPI clients access to your Exchange server and click Next.

Question 2	*What will be automatically created on your Mailbox role after selecting Yes in the previous step?*

16. Review the Readiness Checks page for any errors or warnings. If you have not met the proper software, hardware, and AD requirements, the Readiness Checks page will display errors that describe the component that must be installed or the action that must be taken before you are allowed to continue the Exchange Server 2007 installation. You must then install these components or perform the necessary actions and click Retry to perform the readiness checks again. After you have corrected any IIS errors and have installed the Desktop Experience feature using Server Manager you will only be getting an error about using a 32bit version of Exchange.

17. Click the Install button to begin the Exchange Server 2007 installation. At the end of the Exchange Server 2007 installation, deselect **Finalize installation using the Exchange Management Console** and click Finish. Click OK to close the information window and reboot NT2670Srv##A.

> **NOTE**
> If you receive the following error "An error occurred when executing 'ldifde.exe' to import schema file...", force replication using the repadmin /syncall command and using the Active Directory Sites and Services console on both machines and restart Exchange setup.

> **NOTE**
> If you receive the following error "Service MSExchangeTransport failed to reach status Running", enable IPv6 on the Local Area Connections of both machines and restart Exchange setup.

18. After NT2670Srv##A has rebooted, log in as Administrator.

19. Click Start, All Programs, Microsoft Exchange Server 2007, and then click Exchange Management Console. Click OK to close the dialog box stating that you have unlicensed servers.

20. Highlight Server Configuration in the console tree pane and view NT2670Srv##A in the detail pane. The Role column lists the roles that were successfully installed.

21. Close the Exchange Management Console.

Exercise 7-1-2	Deploying the Second Exchange Server
Overview	In the following exercise, you will install Exchange Server 2007 SP3 Enterprise Edition on NT2670Srv##B with the Mailbox, Hub, and CAS roles as depicted earlier in Figure 7-1-1.
	To complete this lab exercise, NT2670Srv##A and NT2670Srv##B must be started and have network access.
Completion time	60 minutes

1. On NT2670Srv##B, log in as Administrator.

2. Follow the steps that you used in Exercise 7-1-1 to install all components necessary for the proper installation.

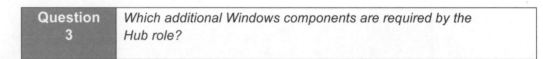

Question 3	Which additional Windows components are required by the Hub role?

3. Click Start and click My Computer. Navigate to the root of the Exchange Server 2007 media and double click the **setup.exe** file.

4. At the Exchange Server 2007 welcome screen, click **Step 4: Install Microsoft Exchange Server 2007 SP3**.

5. At the License Agreement page, select **I accept the terms in the license agreement** and click Next.

6. At the Error Reporting page, ensure that No is selected and click Next.

7. At the Installation Type page, select Custom Exchange Server Installation and click Next.

8. At the Server Role Selection page, select **Mailbox Role**, **Client Access Role**, **Hub Transport Role**, and **Management Tools**. Click Next.

9. At the Client Settings page, select Yes to allow Entourage and Outlook 2003 and earlier MAPI clients access to your Exchange server and click Next.

10. Review the Readiness Checks page for any errors or warnings. If you have not met the proper software, hardware, and AD requirements, the Readiness Checks page will display errors that describe the component that must be installed or the action that must be taken before you are allowed to continue the Exchange Server 2007 installation. You must then install these components or perform the necessary actions and click Retry to perform the readiness checks again.

11. Click the Install button to begin the Exchange Server 2007 installation. At the end of the Exchange Server 2007 installation, deselect **Finalize installation using the Exchange Management Console** and click Finish. Click OK to close the information window and reboot NT2670Srv##B.

12. After NT2670Srv##B has rebooted, log in as Administrator.

13. Click Start, All Programs, Microsoft Exchange Server 2007, and then click Exchange Management Console. Click OK to close the dialog box stating that you have unlicensed servers.

14. Highlight Server Configuration in the console tree pane and view NT2670Srv##B in the detail pane. The Role column lists the roles that were successfully installed.

15. Close the Exchange Management Console.

16. Close all open windows, and log off both computers.

LAB REVIEW: QUESTIONS

Completion time   15 minutes

1. Describe what you learned by completing this lab.

2. Why was it unnecessary to prepare Active Directory during the installation of Exchange Server 2007 on NT2670Srv##B?

3. Briefly outline the additional Windows software components required for the Mailbox, Hub, CAS, UM, and Edge server roles.

Table 7-1-1
Question 3 answer

Server Role	Required Software
Mailbox	
Hub Transport (Hub)	
Client Access Server (CAS)	
Unified Messaging (UM)	
Edge Transport (Edge)	

4. What restriction is set when you select the Edge role during Exchange Server 2007 installation?

5. You are required to specify Entourage and Outlook 2003 and earlier MAPI client support after selecting which server role?

LAB CHALLENGE: PERFORMING AN UNATTENDED EXCHANGE SERVER INSTALLATION

Completion time	35 minutes

You have decided to provide fault tolerance for the UM role within your organization by adding the UM role to NT2670Srv##B. Add the necessary prerequisite software components for the UM role to NT2670Srv##B and perform an unattended (nongraphical) installation of the UM role. Following installation, verify that the role was correctly installed.

LAB 7-2 70-236
CONFIGURING MICROSOFT EXCHANGE SERVER 2007 SP3

This lab contains the following exercises:

Exercise 7-2-1 **Configuring Exchange Administrative Roles**
Exercise 7-2-2 **Configuring the Hub Role**
Exercise 7-2-3 **Configuring the Mailbox Role**
Exercise 7-2-4 **Configuring the CAS Role**
Exercise 7-2-5 **Configuring Send and Receive Connectors**
Exercise 7-2-6 **Configuring an Outlook 2007 Account**
Lab Review: Questions
Lab Challenge: Performing Exchange Server Configuration Using the Exchange Management Shell (Optional)

Estimated lab time: 140 minutes

BEFORE YOU BEGIN

Lab 7-2 assumes that setup has been completed as specified in the setup document and that NT2670Srv##A and NT2670Srv##B have connectivity to the classroom network and the Internet. Moreover, Lab 7-2 assumes that you have completed the exercises in previous Labs.

NOTE	*In this lab, you will see the characters ##. When you see these characters, substitute the two-digit number assigned to your computer.*

SCENARIO

After deploying Exchange Server 2007 within your organization on NT2670Srv##A and NT2670Srv##B, you must configure the Mailbox, CAS, Hub, and Edge roles on each computer.

In the Lab Challenge, you perform server role configuration using cmdlets within the Exchange Management Shell.

After completing this lab, you will be able to:

- Configure Exchange administrative roles

- Configure DNS A and MX Records to support Exchange Server 2007

- Configure the Hub, Edge, Mailbox, and CAS roles on a new Exchange server

- Configure Send and Receive connectors

- Configure Outlook 2007 and Outlook Express email accounts

- Configure Exchange Server roles using cmdlets within the Exchange Management Shell

Exercise 7-2-1   Configuring Exchange Administrative Roles

Overview	After deploying your Exchange servers, you need to configure the appropriate access for Exchange server administrators. While you require complete access to all Exchange servers within your organization, Tom Hurt will need to administer public folders on the Exchange servers within the organization and Lois Lipshitz will need to perform Exchange administration and maintenance on NT2670Srv##B only.
	To complete this lab exercise, NT2670Srv##A and NT2670Srv##B must be started and have network access.
Completion time	5 minutes

1. Turn on your NT2670Srv##A and NT2670Srv##B computers. On the NT2670Srv##A computer, when the logon screen appears, log on using your *Administrator* account and the password *P@ssw0rd*. If the Initial Configuration screen appears, close it.

2. Click Start, All Programs, Microsoft Exchange Server 2007, and then click Exchange Management Console.

3. In the console tree pane, highlight Organization Configuration. View the existing Exchange administrative role assignments in the detail pane.

Question 1	What role is the Administrator user account in the Contoso.com domain granted?

4. In the action pane, click Add Exchange Administrator.

5. At the Add Exchange Administrator window, click the Browse button, select **Tom Hurt**, and click OK.

6. Select **Exchange Public Folder Administrator role** and click Add. At the Completion page, click Finish.

7. In the action pane, click Add Exchange Administrator.

8. At the Add Exchange Administrator window, click the Browse button, select **Lois Lipshitz**, and click OK.

NOTE	If the Lois Lipshitz account does not appear, ensure that it is enabled in the Active Directory Users and Computers console. Her account is in the Production OU.

9. Select **Exchange Server Administrator role** and click the Add button under the Select the server(s) to which this role has access. Select NT2670Srv##B and click OK.

10. Click Add. At the Completion page, click Finish.

11. Leave the Exchange Management Console for the next exercise.

Exercise 7-2-2	Configuring the Hub Role
Overview	Users involved in research and development within the Research department of your organization will be configured with email addresses that have a domain suffix of research.Contoso##.com whereas other users will use email addresses that use the default domain suffix of Contoso##.com. To allow email relay to the users in the Research department, you must configure an accepted domain for research.Contoso##.com on your Hub role servers.
	In addition, for the first few months after Exchange Server 2007 deployment, you want to be notified when there is an email relay problem on your Hub role servers so that you can modify your server and network configuration appropriately. As a result, you will set the postmaster email address to Administrator@Contoso##.com.
	To complete this lab exercise, NT2670Srv##A and NT2670Srv##B must be started and have network access.
Completion time	10 minutes

1. On NT2670Srv##A, in the console tree pane of the Exchange Management Console, expand Organization Configuration and highlight Hub Transport.

2. In the result pane, click the Accepted Domains tab.

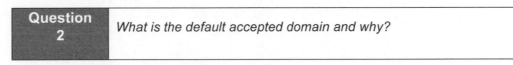

Question 2	What is the default accepted domain and why?

3. In the action pane, click New Accepted Domain.

4. At the New Accepted Domain window type **Research Department Domain** in the Name dialog box. Next, type **research.Contoso##.com** in the Accepted Domain dialog box.

5. Ensure that Authoritative Domain is selected and click New.

6. At the Completion page, click Finish and close the Exchange Management Console.

7. Click Start, All Programs, Microsoft Exchange Server 2007, and then click Exchange Management Shell.

8. Type **Get-TransportServer | Format-List Name,ExternalPostMasterAddress** and press Enter.

Question 3	Is there a postmaster account configured by default?

9.   Type **Set-TransportServer –Identity NT2670Srv##A –ExternalPostMasterAddress Administrator@Contoso##.com** and press Enter.

10. Type **Set-TransportServer –Identity NT2670Srv##B –ExternalPostMasterAddress Administrator@Contoso##.com** and press Enter.

11. Type **Get-TransportServer | Format-List Name,ExternalPostMasterAddress** and press Enter. Verify that the postmaster for your Hub role servers (NT2670Srv##A and NT2670Srv##B) is Administrator@Contoso##.com.

12. Close the Exchange Management Shell.

13. Leave NT2670Srv##A machine logged on for the next exercise.

Exercise 7-2-3	Configuring the Mailbox Role
Overview	As part of your Mailbox role configuration, you wish to move the location of the default storage groups, mailbox databases, and public folder databases on NT2670Srv##A and NT2670Srv##B. Although you would normally move these to another hard disk or RAID array in a production environment, you will move them to directories under the root of C:\ on each Mailbox role server. In addition, you will create additional storage groups and mailbox databases as well as set storage limits on the mailbox and public folder databases on NT2670Srv##A and NT2670Srv##B. To complete this lab exercise, NT2670Srv##A and NT2670Srv##B must be started and have network access.
Completion time	40 minutes

1. On NT2670Srv##A, create the following folders on your C drive: C:\SG1, C:\SG2, and C:\SG3 folders.

2. On NT2670Srv##B, log in as Administrator. Create the following folders on your C drive: C:\SG1, C:\SG2, and C:\SG3 folders.

3. On NT2670Srv##A click Start, All Programs, Microsoft Exchange Server 2007, and then click Exchange Management Console. The Exchange Management Console window appears.

4. In the console tree pane, expand Server Configuration and highlight Mailbox.

5. In the detail pane, highlight NT2670Srv##A. View the storage groups in the work pane. Expand them to view the databases within.

6. In the detail pane, highlight NT2670Srv##B. View the storage groups in the work pane. Expand them to view the databases within. If NT2670Srv##B does not have a Second Storage Group that contains a Public Folder database, you will create them later in this exercise.

Question 4	*What storage groups and databases are configured by default on NT2670Srv##A and NT2670Srv##B?*

7. In the detail pane, highlight NT2670Srv##A and select the First Storage Group in the work pane.

8. In the action pane, click Move Storage Group Path.

9. At the Move Storage Group Path window, click Browse beside the Log files path dialog box, select **C:\SG1**, and click OK.

10. Beside the System files path dialog box, click Browse, select **C:\SG1**, and click OK.

11. Click Move. When prompted to confirm that databases within the storage group will be unavailable during the move operation, click Yes.

12. Click Finish at the Completion page to close the Move Storage Group Path window.

13. In the work pane, highlight Second Storage Group.

14. In the action pane, click Move Storage Group Path.

15. At the Move Storage Group Path window, click Browse beside the Log files path dialog box, select **C:\SG2**, and click OK.

16. Beside the System files path dialog box, click Browse, select **C:\SG2**, and click OK.

17. Click Move. When prompted to confirm that databases within the storage group will be unavailable during the move operation, click Yes. The Completion page appears.

18. Click Finish at the Completion page to close the Move Storage Group Path window.

19. In the work pane, highlight Mailbox Database under the First Storage Group.

20. In the action pane, click Move Database Path.

21. At the Move Database Path window, click Browse beside the Database file path dialog box, select **C:\SG1**, and click Save.

22. Click Move. When prompted to confirm that the database will be unavailable during the move operation, click Yes.

23. Click Finish to at the Completion page to close the Move Database Path window.

24. In the work pane, highlight Public Folder Database.

25. In the action pane, click Move Database Path.

26. At the Move Database Path window, click Browse beside the Database file path dialog box, select **C:\SG2**, and click Save.

27. Click Move. When prompted to confirm that the database will be unavailable during the move operation, click Yes.

28. Click Finish at the Completion page to close the Move Database Path window.

29. On the NT2670Srv##B computer, log on using your *Administrator* account and the password *P@ssw0rd*. If the Initial Configuration screen appears, close it. Using the same procedure outlined in Steps 7 to 28, move the default storage groups and databases to C:\SG1 and C:\SG2 on NT2670Srv##B. If NT2670Srv##B does not have a Second Storage Group that contains a Public Folder database, you will create them later in this exercise.

30. On the NT2670Srv##A computer, highlight NT2670Srv##A in the Exchange Management Console detail pane.

31. In the action pane, click New Storage Group.

32. At the New Storage Group window type **Third Storage Group** in the Storage group name field.

33. Beside the Log files path dialog box, click Browse, select **C:\SG3**, and click OK.

34. Beside the System files path dialog box, click Browse, select **C:\SG3**, and click OK.

35. Click New. Click Finish at the Completion page to close the New Storage Group window.

36. In the work pane, highlight Third Storage Group and click New Mailbox Database in the action pane.

37. At the New Mailbox Database window, type **Second Mailbox Database** in the Mailbox database name field. Beside the Database file path dialog box, click Browse select **C:\SG3**, and click OK.

38. Verify that Mount this database is selected to ensure that the database will be available for use after creation and click New.

39. Click Finish at the Completion page to close the New Mailbox Database window.

40. On the NT2670Srv##B computer, highlight NT2670Srv##B in the Exchange Management Console detail pane. Using the same procedure outlined in Steps 31 to 39, create a new storage group called **Third Storage Group** as well as a mailbox database called **Second Mailbox Database**. All storage group and database files should reside in **C:\SG3** on NT2670Srv##B. If NT2670Srv##B does not have a Second Storage Group that contains a Public Folder database, create it using the same process outlined in Steps 31 to 40 (select New Public Folder Database instead of New Mailbox Database). The Second Storage Group and Public Folder database should store files in the C:\SG2 directory on NT2670Srv##B.

41. On the NT2670Srv##A computer, highlight NT2670Srv##A in the Exchange Management Console detail pane.

42. In the work pane, highlight the Mailbox Database under the First Storage Group and click Properties in the action pane.

43. Highlight the Limits tab and configure the following limits:

   • Issue warning at 409600 KB (400 MB)

   • Prohibit send at 460800 KB (450 MB)

   • Prohibit send and receive at 512000 KB (500 MB)

- Warning message interval: Run daily at 2:00 a.m.

44. Click OK when finished.

45. In the work pane, highlight the Public Folder Database under the Second Storage Group and click Properties in the action pane.

46. Highlight the Limits tab and configure the following limits:

   - Issue warning at 102400 KB (100 MB)

   - Prohibit post at 122880 KB (120 MB)

   - Maximum item size of 15360 KB (15 MB)

   - Warning message interval: Run daily at 2:00 a.m.

47. On the NT2670Srv##B computer, highlight NT2670Srv##B in the Exchange Management Console detail pane. Using the same procedure outlined in Steps 42 to 46, configure the same storage limits on the Mailbox Database and Public Folder Database on NT2670Srv##B.

48. Leave both machines logged on for the next exercise.

Exercise 7-2-4	Configuring the CAS Role
Overview	Your organization plans to allow email access to POP3, IMAP4, Outlook Anywhere, and Outlook Web Access (OWA) clients. To ensure security for OWA, file server access will not be allowed for OWA users from a public computer. To complete this lab exercise, NT2670Srv##A and NT2670Srv##B must be started and have network access.
Completion time	15 minutes

1. On NT2670Srv##A, click Start, All Programs, Administrative Tools, and then click Services.

2. At the Services console, right click Microsoft Exchange IMAP4 in the right pane and click Properties. Select Automatic in the Startup type drop-down box and click Apply. Next, click Start and click OK.

3. At the Services console, right click Microsoft Exchange POP3 in the right pane and click Properties. Select Automatic in the Startup type drop-down box and click Apply. Next, click Start and click OK.

4. Close the Services console.

5. Open the Exchange Management Console. In the console tree pane, expand Server Configuration and highlight Client Access.

6. In the action pane, click Enable Outlook Anywhere.

7. At the Enable Outlook Anywhere window, type **NT2670Srv##A.Contoso##.com** in the External host name field. Select NTLM authentication and click Enable.

8. Click Finish at the Completion screen.

9. In the work pane, highlight owa (Default Web Site) under the Outlook Web Access tab and click Properties in the action pane.

10. Highlight the Remote File Servers tab. Select Allow in the drop-down box and click Configure. In the Internal Domain Suffix List window, type **Contoso##.com** in the dialog box, click Add, and then click OK.

Question 5	*What file servers are OWA clients allowed to connect to?*

11. Highlight the Private Computer File Access tab and ensure that the following items are selected (enabled):

- Enable direct file access

- Enable WebReady Document Viewing

- Windows File Shares

- Windows SharePoint Services

12. Highlight the Public Computer File Access tab and ensure that the following items are deselected (disabled) and click OK:

- Enable direct file access

- Enable WebReady Document Viewing

- Windows File Shares

- Windows SharePoint Services

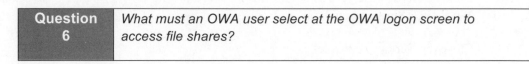

Question 6	What must an OWA user select at the OWA logon screen to access file shares?

13. On NT2670Srv##B, log in as Administrator.

14. Using the same procedure outlined in Steps 1 to 12, configure the POP3 and IMAP4 services to start automatically, enable Outlook Anywhere using an external host name of **NT2670Srv##B.Contoso##.com**, and configure OWA to allow access to all file servers and features from a private computer only.

15. Leave both machines logged on for the next exercise.

Exercise 7-2-5	**Configuring Send and Receive Connectors**
Overview	Although the default Send and Receive connectors on your Hub and Edge role servers provide for email relay and connections from POP3 and IMAP4 clients, your organization has some additional connector needs.
	First, the Macintosh IMAP email clients within your organization will be configured to send SMTP email to NT2670Srv##A using port 1587 and TLS authentication. As a result, you will need to configure a receive connector on NT2670Srv##A that allows for connections.
	In addition, you wish to ensure that any emails sent to recipients in the hotmail.com, gmail.com, and yahoo.com domains are no larger than 512 KB. To do this, you must create a send connector that applies to your Edge role server that provides the appropriate restrictions.
	To complete this lab exercise, NT2670Srv##A and NT2670Srv##B must be started and have network access.
Completion time	10 minutes

1. On NT2670Srv##A, in the Exchange Management Console window, expand Server Configuration in the console tree, click Hub Transport, and highlight NT2670Srv##A in the result pane.

Question 7	*What two receive connectors are configured by default on NT2670Srv##A and what purpose do they serve?*

2. In the action pane, click New Receive Connector.

3. At the New SMTP Receive Connector window, type **Macintosh IMAP Clients** in the Name field, select Custom from the Select the intended use for this Receive connector drop-down box, and click Next.

4. At the Local Network settings page, type **NT2670Srv##A.Contoso##.com** in the dialog box at the bottom of the screen and click Edit.

5. At the Edit Receive Connector Binding window, type **1587** in the Port dialog box and click OK.

6. Click Next. At the Remote Network settings page click Next.

7. Review your selections and click New. Click Finish to close the New SMTP Receive Connector window.

8. In the work pane, highlight Macintosh IMAP Clients and click Properties in the action pane.

9. Highlight the Authentication tab and ensure that Transport Layer Security (TLS) is selected. Next, highlight the Permission Groups tab and ensure that Exchange users is selected. Click OK when finished.

10. Expand Organization Configuration in the console tree, highlight Hub Transport, and click the Send Connectors tab in the result pane.

11. In the action pane, click New Send Connector.

12. At the New SMTP Send Connector window type **Hotmail, Gmail, and Yahoo Mail** in the Name field. In the Select the intended use for this Send connector drop-down box, ensure that Internet is selected and click Next.

13. At the Address space page, click Add, type **hotmail.com** in the Address dialog box, select Include all subdomains, and click OK.

14. Click Add again, type **gmail.com** in the Address dialog box, type **2** in the Cost dialog box, select Include all subdomains, and click OK.

15. Click Add again, type **yahoo.com** in the Address dialog box, type **3** in the Cost dialog box, select Include all subdomains, and click OK.

16. Click Next. At the Network settings page, click Next.

17. At the Source Server page, click Next. Review your selections and click New.

18. Click Finish to close the New SMTP Send Connector window.

19. Highlight the Hotmail, Gmail, and Yahoo Mail send connector under the Send Connectors tab in the detail pane and click Properties in the action pane.

20. On the General tab of send connector properties, type **512** in the Maximum message size (KB) dialog box and click OK.

21. Leave both machines logged on for the next exercise.

Exercise 7-2-6   Configuring an Outlook 2007 Account

Overview	To test various Exchange Server 2007 functionalities in this lab manual, you will need to set up a MAPI account within Outlook 2007. In this lab exercise, you will use your Windows 7 machine and configure an Exchange (MAPI) email account for yourself (Administrator).
	To complete this lab exercise, NT2670Srv##A must be started and have network access.
Completion time	20 minutes

1. On NT2670Srv##A, in the Exchange Management Console window, expand Recipient Configuration in the console tree, click Mailbox. Ensure that a Mailbox has been created for Administrator.

2. Turn on Workstation##, log in as Contoso99\Administrator. Click Start, All Programs, Microsoft Office, and then click Microsoft Office Outlook 2007. If the Office 2007 Startup wizard appears, click Next. Select No and click Next. Select Continue with no e-mail support and click Finish. Close Outlook 2007.

3. Click Start, Control Panel, User Accounts, Mail. At the Mail Setup—Outlook window, click E-mail Accounts. If prompted to enable RSS feeds, click Yes.

4. In the Account Settings window, click New.

5. At the Add New E-mail Account window select Manually configure server settings or additional server types and click Next.

6. At the Choose E-mail Service page select Microsoft Exchange and click Next.

7. Type **NT2670Srv##A.Contoso##.com** in the Microsoft Exchange Server dialog box, deselect **Use Cached Exchange Mode**, type **Administrator** in the User Name dialog box, and click Check Name. After the Exchange server and user names are underlined, click Next.

 If you receive an error stating that your machine does not have a Default Gateway set, use the Network and Sharing Center to assign a Default Gateway of 172.16.##.1 and try again.

8. At the Congratulations! screen, click Finish to close the Add New E-mail Account window.

9. Close the Mail Setup   Outlook window.

10. Click Start, All Programs, Microsoft Office, and then click Microsoft Office Outlook 2007. Verify that Outlook 2007 opens without errors and close Outlook 2007.

LAB REVIEW QUESTIONS

Completion time	15 minutes

1. Describe what you learned by completing this lab.

2. Does it matter what Mail server priority number is chosen in Exercise 7-2-2? Explain.

3. In Exercise 7-2-3, explain why you should configure the postmaster account to a different user account (not Administrator@Contoso##.com) after a few months in a production environment.

4. Why was it unnecessary to import the Edge subscription file into NT2670Srv##B during Exercise 7-2-4?

5. In Exercise 7-2-5, you configured your storage groups and databases to reside on C:\. Explain why this is poor practice in a production environment.

6. Why should you restrict access to file shares and documents for OWA users?

7. Why are the POP3 and IMAP4 services disabled by default?

LAB CHALLENGE: PERFORMING EXCHANGE SERVER CONFIGURATION USING THE EXCHANGE MANAGEMENT SHELL (OPTIONAL)

Completion time	25 minutes

Although you have configured NT2670Srv##A and NT2670Srv##B using the Exchange Management Console in Exercise 7-2-1, and 7-2-3 through 7-2-7, you can also perform Exchange server configuration using cmdlets within the Exchange Management Shell.

Use the Exchange Management Shell to perform the following additional configuration tasks on your Exchange servers:

- Configure Celine DeVries as an Exchange View-Only Administrator.

- Ensure that email sent to recipients with a domain suffix of marketing.Contoso.com domain will be processed by your Hub role servers and sent to the appropriate mailboxes in Contoso.com.

- Create a new storage group called Fourth Storage Group on NT2670Srv##B that contains a mailbox database called Third Mailbox Database. All files for the storage group and database should reside in the C:\SG4 folder.

- Set the following limits on the Third Mailbox Database:

    o Issue warning at 409600 KB (400 MB)

    o Prohibit send at 460800 KB (450 MB)

    o Prohibit send and receive at 512000 KB (500 MB)

- Ensure that any outgoing Internet email to recipients in the rocketmail.com domain are limited to 1 MB in size

LAB 8-1 70-236
CONFIGURING RECIPIENT OBJECTS

This lab contains the following exercises:

Exercise 8-1-1 Configuring Mailbox Users
Exercise 8-1-2 Providing Unique Mailbox User Configuration
Exercise 8-1-3 Configuring Mailbox User Permissions
Exercise 8-1-4 Configuring Mail Users
Exercise 8-1-5 Configuring Mail Contacts
Exercise 8-1-6 Configuring Mail-Enabled Groups
Exercise 8-1-7 Configuring Resource Mailboxes
Exercise 8-1-8 Moving Mailboxes
Lab Review: Questions
Lab Challenge: Configuring Recipients Using the Exchange Management Shell

Estimated lab time: 185 minutes

BEFORE YOU BEGIN

Lab 8-1 assumes that setup has been completed as specified in the setup document and that NT2670Srv##A and NT2670Srv##B have connectivity to the classroom network and the Internet. Moreover, 8-1 assumes that you have completed the exercises in previous labs.

| NOTE | *In this lab, you will see the characters ##. When you see these characters, substitute the two-digit number assigned to your computer.* |

SCENARIO

Now that you have configured the necessary server roles on the Exchange servers within your organization, you can create recipient objects to represent the users within your organization. In this lab, you will create and configure mailbox users, mail users, mail contacts, mail-enabled groups, and resource mailboxes. In addition, you will configure mailbox permissions, move mailboxes, and disable and reconnect a mailbox.

In the Lab Challenge, you will perform recipient object configuration using cmdlets within the Exchange Management Shell.

After completing this lab, you will be able to:

- Create and configure mailbox users
- Configure mailbox user permissions
- Create and configure mail users
- Create and configure mail contacts
- Create and configure mail-enabled universal distribution groups
- Create and configure mail-enabled dynamic distribution groups
- Create and configure resource mailboxes
- Move mailboxes
- Disconnect and reconnect mailboxes
- Configure recipient objects using cmdlets within the Exchange Management Shell

Exercise 8-1-1   Configuring Mailbox Users

Overview	In this Lab Exercise, you will configure mailboxes for the Active Directory users that you created in Lab 6-1. In addition, you will set common configuration parameters including protocol support, messaging restrictions, and current project (using a custom attribute).
	To complete this lab exercise, NT2670Srv##A and NT2670Srv##B must be started and have network access.
Completion time	40 minutes

1. Turn on your NT2670Srv##A and NT2670Srv##B computers. On the NT2670Srv##A computer, when the logon screen appears, log on using your *Administrator* account and the password *P@ssw0rd*. If the Initial Configuration screen appears, close it.

2. Click Start, All Programs, Microsoft Exchange Server 2007, and then click Exchange Management Console.

3. In the console tree pane, expand Recipient Configuration and highlight Mailbox.

4. In the action pane, click New Mailbox.

5. At the New Mailbox window, select User Mailbox and click Next.

6. At the User Type page, select Existing users, click the Add button, select Sophia Boren, click OK and click Next.

7. At the Mailbox Settings page, ensure that sophia.boren is listed in the Alias dialog box.

Question 1	*What internal email address will be used for Sophia Boren by default?*

8. Click Browse next to the Mailbox database dialog box, select the Mailbox Database in the First Storage Group on NT2670Srv##A and click OK.

9. Click Next. Review the summary of your settings and click New.

10. Click Finish to close the New Mailbox window.

11. Highlight Sophia Boren in the detail pane and select Properties from the action pane.

12. On the General tab of user properties, click Custom Attributes, type **Project58** in the Custom attribute 1 dialog box and click OK.

13. Select the Mailbox Features tab, highlight POP3, and click Disable. Next, highlight IMAP4 and click Disable.

14. Select the Mail Flow Settings tab, highlight Delivery Options, and click Properties. Select Maximum recipients, enter 100 in the associated dialog box, and click OK.

15. Highlight Message Size Restrictions and click Properties. Under the Sending message size section, Select Maximum message size (in KB) and enter 10240 in the associated dialog box. Under the Receiving message size section, Select Maximum message size (in KB) and enter 20480 in the associated dialog box. Click OK.

16. Click OK to close mailbox user properties.

17. Using the same procedure outlined in Steps 4 to 16, configure the other mailbox users listed in Table 8-1-1 with the appropriate settings.

Table 8-1-1
Mailbox user configuration information

User Name	Custom Attribute 1	Enabled Protocols	Maximum Recipients	Maximum Send Message Size	Maximum Receive Message Size
Sophia Boren	Project58	OWA, ActiveSync, MAPI	100	10240	20480
Mel Booker	Project45	OWA, ActiveSync, MAPI, POP3	50	20480	20480
Celine DeVries	Project58	OWA, ActiveSync, MAPI, IMAP4	100	10240	20480
Mark Daly	Project58	OWA, MAPI	100	10240	20480
Tiger Smith	Project45	OWA, ActiveSync, MAPI, IMAP4	50	20480	20480
Meg Roombas	Project58	OWA, ActiveSync, MAPI, IMAP4	100	10240	20480
Jacques Guillere	Project45	OWA, MAPI, POP3	50	20480	20480
Juan Ton	Project45	OWA, ActiveSync, MAPI	50	20480	20480
Sarah Parkers	Project45	OWA, ActiveSync, MAPI, POP3	50	20480	20480
Lois Lipshitz	Project45	OWA, ActiveSync, MAPI, IMAP4	50	20480	20480

Jessica Augustus	Project58	OWA, ActiveSync, MAPI, POP3	100	10240	20480
Tom Hurt	Project58	OWA, ActiveSync, MAPI	100	10240	20480
Bernadette Jones	Project58	OWA, MAPI	100	10240	20480
Jennifer Coupland	Project45	OWA, ActiveSync, MAPI	50	20480	20480
Lisa Lackner	Project45	OWA, ActiveSync, MAPI	50	20480	20480
Mathew Kropf	Project45	OWA, ActiveSync, MAPI, IMAP4	50	20480	20480
Matt Adams	Project58	OWA, ActiveSync, MAPI	100	10240	20480
David Schwan	Project58	OWA, MAPI,	100	10240	20480

Exercise 8-1-2   Providing Unique Mailbox User Configuration

Overview	Over time, you will need to provide custom configuration for individual mailbox users to match the needs of the user and organization. In this Lab Exercise, you will provide unique configuration for three mailbox users.
	Mel Booker is the Human Resources Manager and should receive any email sent to HR@Contoso##.com. In addition, Mel Booker accesses his email from a portable wireless device using POP3 that requires plain text formatted email.
	Tom Hurt manages the Production department. While Tom is away on vacation, his supervisor Jennifer Coupland will be performing his duties. As a result, you must ensure that copies of any emails sent to Tom Hurt will be forwarded to Jennifer Coupland.
	David Schwan sends emails to the other production team on a regular basis but often sends emails to Matt Adams in the Sales department instead of Matthew Kropf in the Production department. To prevent this, you will configure Matt Adams' mailbox to reject email from David Schwan.
	To complete this lab exercise, NT2670Srv##A and NT2670Srv##B must be started and have network access.
Completion time	10 minutes

1. On NT2670Srv##A, in the console tree pane of the Exchange Management Console, expand Recipient Configuration and highlight Mailbox.

2. Highlight Mel Booker in the detail pane and select Properties from the action pane.

3. Click the E-Mail Addresses tab and deselect **Automatically update e-mail addresses based on e-mail address policy**. Click Add and type **HR@Contoso##.com** in the E-mail address dialog box of the SMTP Address window and click OK.

4. Click the Mailbox Features tab, highlight POP3, and select Properties. Deselect **Use protocol default**, select Text from the drop-down box, and click OK.

5. Click OK to close mailbox user properties.

6. Highlight Tom Hurt in the detail pane and select Properties from the action pane.

7. Click the Mail Flow Settings tab, highlight Delivery Options, and click Properties. Select **Forward to**, click Browse, highlight Jennifer Coupland, and click OK. Select **Deliver message to both forwarding address and mailbox** and click OK.

8. Click OK to close mailbox user properties.

9. Highlight Matt Adams in the detail pane and select Properties from the action pane.

10. Click the Mail Flow Settings tab, highlight Message Delivery Restrictions, and click Properties. Under the **Reject messages from** section, click **Senders in the following list** and click Add. Select David Schwan and click OK. Click OK to return to mailbox user properties.

11. Click OK to close mailbox user properties.

Exercise 8-1-3	Configuring Mailbox User Permissions
Overview	Understanding when to configure and use Send as, Send on behalf, and Full access permissions with mailbox users is vital for any Exchange administrator. In this Lab Exercise, you will configure the different mailbox permissions on the Tiger Smith mailbox user and test your permissions assignments afterwards. To complete this lab exercise, NT2670Srv##A and NT2670Srv##B must be started and have network access.
Completion time	15 minutes

1. On NT2670Srv##A, in the console tree pane of the Exchange Management Console, expand Recipient Configuration and highlight Mailbox.

2. In the result pane, highlight Tiger Smith and click Properties from the action pane.

3. Click the Mail Flow Settings tab, highlight Delivery Options, and click Properties. Under the Send on behalf section, click Add, highlight Administrator, and click OK. Click OK to return to mailbox user properties.

4. Click OK to close mailbox user properties.

Question 2	What does Send on behalf permission allow Administrator to do as Tiger Smith?

5. In the result pane, highlight Tiger Smith and click Manage Send As Permission in the action pane.

6. At the Manage Send As Permission window, click Add, select Administrator, and click OK. Click Manage.

7. Click Finish to close the Manage Send As Permission window.

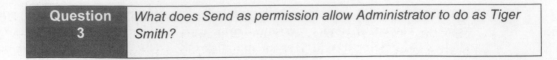

8.   In the result pane, highlight Tiger Smith and click Manage Full Access Permission in the action pane.

9.   At the Manage Full Access Permission window, click Add, select Administrator, and click OK. Click Manage.

10.   Click Finish to close the Manage Full Access Permission window.

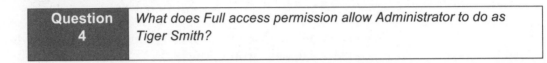

11.   Turn on Workstation##, log in as Contoso99\Administrator. Click Start, All Programs, Microsoft Office, and then click Microsoft Office Outlook 2007.

12.   Click the Tools menu and select Account Settings.

Depending on the version of Outlook you are using, Account Settings may be under the File menu and some instructions may be different.

13.   Highlight Administrator@Contoso##.com under the E-mail tab and click Change.

14.   At the Change E-mail Account window, click More Settings.

15.   At the Microsoft Exchange window, highlight the Advanced tab and click the Add button. Type **Tiger Smith** and click OK.

Question 5	Why are you allowed to add Tiger Smith's mailbox to Administrator's Outlook account settings?

16.   Click OK to return to the Change E-mail Account window and click Next. Click Finish to close the Change E-mail Account window and click Close to close the Account Settings window.

17.   In the left pane of Outlook 2007, expand Mailbox—Tiger Smith and highlight Inbox.

18. Click New to compose a new email. At the new message window, click the Options tab click the From button, click the From drop down box and select other email address and browse to select Tiger Smith. Next, click the To button and select Administrator.

19. Type **Permissions Test** in the Subject field and click the Send button.

20. Expand Mailbox—Administrator in the left pane of Outlook 2007 and highlight Inbox. Double click the email from Tiger Smith.

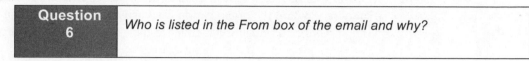

Question 6	Who is listed in the From box of the email and why?

21. Close your email and close Outlook 2007.

Exercise 8-1-4   Configuring Mail Users

Overview	To provide effective marketing for your company's products, you have hired two marketing specialists from a marketing agency: Courtney Davies and Mike Moritz. Courtney and Mike will be working alongside the rest of your Marketing department for the next six months and will require domain access but will not require a mailbox because they already have a mailbox at their home organization. To facilitate Courtney and Mike, you will need to configure mail users for them so that others within the organization can easily locate them within the Global Address List and send email to their external email address.
	To complete this lab exercise, NT2670Srv##A and NT2670Srv##B must be started and have network access.
Completion time	10 minutes

1. On NT2670Srv##A, in the console tree pane of the Exchange Management Console, expand Recipient Configuration and highlight Mail Contact.

2. In the action pane, click New Mail User.

3. At the New Mail User window, select Existing user, click the Browse button, select Courtney Davies in the Select User window that appears and click OK. Click Next.

4. At the Mail Settings page, ensure that courtney.davies is listed in the Alias dialog box.

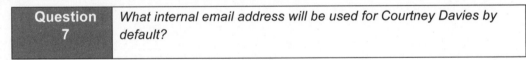

Question 7	What internal email address will be used for Courtney Davies by default?

5. Click Edit next to the External e-mail address dialog box, type **cdavies@marketinghorizons.com** in the SMTP Address window that appears and click OK.

6. Click Next. Review the summary of your settings and click New.

7. Click Finish to close the New Mail User window.

8. Highlight Courtney Davies in the detail pane and select Properties from the action pane.

9. On the General tab of mail user properties, click Custom Attributes, type **Project45** in the Custom attribute 1 dialog box and click OK.

10. Select the Mail Flow Settings tab, highlight Message Size Restrictions, and click Properties. Under the Receiving message size section, Select Maximum message size (in KB) and enter **10240** in the associated dialog box. Click OK.

11. Click OK to close mail user properties.

12. Using the same procedure outlined in Steps 2 to 11, configure a mail user for the existing Mike Moritz user account that uses an alias of **mike.moritz** and an external email address of **mikem@gnumarketing.org**. For the Mike Moritz mail user, ensure that Custom attribute 1 is set to Project58 and that the maximum receiving message size is set to 10240 KB.

Exercise 8-1-5   Configuring Mail Contacts

Overview	Your organization employs two contract janitorial workers. Joe Mos is the daytime janitorial worker and Judy Chong is the nighttime janitorial worker. Since Joe and Judy have existing email accounts on an external email system and do not need domain access, you will create mail contacts for them to ensure that users within your organization can send special cleanup requests as necessary. Since these requests will be simple, you wish to ensure that they are not sent in MAPI rich text and are less than 1024 KB (1 MB).
	To complete this lab exercise, NT2670Srv##A and NT2670Srv##B must be started and have network access.
Completion time	10 minutes

1. On NT2670Srv##A, in the console tree pane of the Exchange Management Console, expand Recipient Configuration and highlight Mail Contact.

2. In the action pane, click New Mail Contact.

3. At the New Mail Contact window, ensure that New contact is selected and click Next.

4. At the Contact Information page, click Browse, select the Production OU, and click OK.

5. Type **Joe** in the First name dialog box, type **Mos** in the Last name dialog box and type **joe.mos** in the Alias dialog box.

6. Click Edit next to the External e-mail address dialog box, type **joemos@cleanupsolutions.com** in the SMTP Address window and click OK.

7. Click Next. Review the summary of your settings and click New.

8. Click Finish to close the New Mail Contact window.

9. Select the Joe Mos mail contact in the detail pane and click Properties in the action pane.

10. In the Use MAPI rich text format window, select Never from the drop-down box.

11. Select the Mail Flow Settings tab, highlight Message Size Restrictions, and click Properties. Under the Receiving message size section, select Maximum message size (in KB) and enter **1024** in the associated dialog box. Click OK.

12. Click OK to close mail contact properties.

13. Using the same procedure outlined in Steps 2 to 12, configure a mail contact for Judy Chong in the Production OU that uses an alias of **judy.chong** and an external email address of **judyc@tps.org**. For the Judy Chong mail contact, ensure that MAPI rich text format is disabled, and that the maximum receiving message size is set to 1024 KB.

Exercise 8-1-6   Configuring Mail-Enabled Groups

Overview	Certain messages within your organization must be relayed to all project managers or project members. As a result, you plan to implement mail-enabled groups to simplify sending email to multiple recipients.
	Because there are only three project managers and these project managers often require special permissions on resources, you plan to create a mail-enabled universal security group with the email alias Project-Managers@Contoso##.com. For project members, you plan to create two dynamic distribution groups that search for the appropriate custom attribute within the recipient objects in your domain. Users should be able to email Project45@Contoso##.com and Project58@Contoso##.com to relay email to the appropriate project members.
	To complete this lab exercise, NT2670Srv##A and NT2670Srv##B must be started and have network access.
Completion time	15 minutes

1. On NT2670Srv##A, in the console tree pane of the Exchange Management Console, expand Recipient Configuration and highlight Distribution Group.

2. In the action pane, click New Distribution Group.

3. At the New Distribution Group window, ensure that New group is selected and click Next.

4. At the Group Information page, select Security in the Group type section. Next, click Browse, select the Contoso##.com domain, and click OK. Type **Project-Managers** in the Name dialog box and note that the preWindows 2000 name and alias are given the same value.

5. Click Next. Review the summary of your settings and click New.

6. Click Finish to close the New Distribution Group window.

7. Select the Project-Managers group in the detail pane and click Properties in the action pane.

8. Highlight the Members tab and click Add. Hold down the Ctrl key on your keyboard; select Sophia Boren, Tiger Smith, and Tom Hurt; and click OK.

9. Click OK again to close the properties of the mail-enabled universal security group.

10. In the action pane, click New Dynamic Distribution Group.

11. At the New Dynamic Distribution Group window click Browse, select the Contoso##.com domain, and click OK.

12. Next, type **Project58** in the Name dialog box and note that the same value is automatically placed in the Alias dialog box. Click Next.

13. At the Filter Settings page click Browse, select Contoso##.com, and click OK.

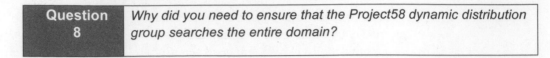

| Question 8 | Why did you need to ensure that the Project58 dynamic distribution group searches the entire domain? |

14. Click Next. Select **Custom Attribute 1 equals Value** in the **Step 1: Select condition(s)** dialog box. Next, click **specified** in the **Step 2: Edit the condition(s) dialog box**, type **Project58**, click Add, and then click OK.

15. Perform a test search for all recipients within your domain with the first custom attribute set to Project58 by clicking Preview. Click OK when finished and click Next.

16. Review the summary of your settings and click New.

17. Click Finish to close the New Dynamic Distribution Group window.

18. Using the same procedure outlined in Steps 10 to 17, create another dynamic distribution group called Project45 under Contoso##.com that includes all recipient objects within Contoso##.com with the first custom attribute set to Project45.

19. On Workstation##, log in as Contoso99\Administrator. Click Start, All Programs, Microsoft Office, and then click Microsoft Office Outlook 2007.

20. Click New to compose a new email. In the To dialog box, type **Project-Managers@Contoso##.com**. Next, type **Project-Managers Group Email Test** in the Subject dialog box and click Send.

21. Click New to compose a new email. In the To dialog box, type **Project45@Contoso##.com**. Next, type **Project45 Group Email Test** in the Subject dialog box and click Send.

22. Click New to compose a new email. In the To dialog box, type **Project58@Contoso##.com**. Next, type **Project58 Group Email Test** in the Subject dialog box and click Send.

23. Expand Mailbox—Tiger Smith and highlight Inbox.

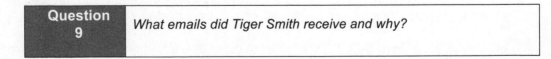

| Question 9 | What emails did Tiger Smith receive and why? |

24. Close Outlook 2007.

Exercise 8-1-7   Configuring Resource Mailboxes

Overview	Your organization plans to use the resource scheduling abilities of Outlook to book conference rooms for meetings as well as book the use of a presentation SmartBoard without the use of a delegate to oversee the process. As a result, you must create and configure the appropriate resource mailboxes, enable automatic booking, and configure a book-in policy that does not require a delegate when resource conflicts arise. To complete this lab exercise, NT2670Srv##A and NT2670Srv##B must be started and have network access.
Completion time	25 minutes

1. On NT2670Srv##A, click Start, All Programs, Microsoft Exchange Server 2007, and then click Exchange Management Shell.

2. At the Exchange Management Shell prompt, type **Set-ResourceConfig - ResourcePropertySchema** (**'Room/Projector','Room/Whiteboard','Room/WiFi'**) and press Enter.

3. In the console tree pane of the Exchange Management Console, expand Recipient Configuration and highlight Mailbox.

4. In the action pane, click New Mailbox.

5. At the New Mailbox window, select Equipment Mailbox and click Next.

6. At the User Type page, ensure that New user is selected and click Next.

7. Type **SmartBoard** in the Name dialog box, type **SmartBoard** in the User logon name dialog box, and click Next.

8. At the Mailbox Settings page, ensure that the Alias dialog box contains SmartBoard.

9. Click Browse next to the Mailbox database dialog box, select the Mailbox Database in the First Storage Group on NT2670Srv##A, and click OK.

10. Click Next. Review the summary of your settings and click New.

11. Click Finish to close the New Mailbox window.

12. Highlight SmartBoard in the detail pane and click Properties in the action pane.

13. Select the Resource Information tab, type **1** in the Resource capacity dialog box, and click OK to close the properties of the resource mailbox.

14. In the action pane, click New Mailbox.

15. At the New Mailbox window, select Room Mailbox and click Next.

16. At the User Type page, ensure that New user is selected and click Next.

17. Type **ConferenceRoom1** in the Name dialog box, type **ConferenceRoom1** in the User logon name dialog box, and click Next.

18. At the Mailbox Settings page, ensure that the Alias dialog box contains ConferenceRoom1.

19. Click Browse next to the Mailbox database dialog box, select the Mailbox Database in the First Storage Group on NT2670Srv##A, and click OK.

20. Click Next. Review the summary of your settings and click New.

21. Click Finish to close the New Mailbox window.

22. Highlight ConferenceRoom1 in the detail pane and click Properties in the action pane.

23. Select the Resource Information tab and type **10** in the Resource capacity dialog box. Next, click Add. While holding down the Ctrl key on your keyboard, select Projector and WiFi, and click OK.

24. Click OK to close the properties of the resource mailbox.

25. Using the same procedure outlined in Steps 14 to 24, create and configure the resource mailboxes listed in Table 8-1-2.

Table 8-1-2
Resource mailbox configuration information

Resource Mailbox Name	Capacity	Resources
ConferenceRoom1	10	Projector, WiFi
ConferenceRoom2	25	Projector, Whiteboard, WiFi
ConferenceRoom3	10	Projector, Whiteboard
ConferenceRoom4	15	Projector, Whiteboard, WiFi
ConferenceRoom5	18	Whiteboard

26. At the Exchange Management Shell prompt, type **Set-MailboxCalendarSettings –Identity 'ConferenceRoom1' –AutomateProcessing:AutoAccept** and press Enter to enable automatic booking on the ConferenceRoom1 resource mailbox.

27. At the Exchange Management Shell prompt, type **Set-MailboxCalendarSettings –Identity 'ConferenceRoom1' –AllBookInPolicy:$true** and press Enter to specify a book-in policy for the ConferenceRoom1 resource mailbox for all users.

28. Using the procedure outlined in the previous two steps, enable automatic booking and specify a book-in policy for all other resource mailboxes.

29. Close the Exchange Management Shell.

30. Turn on Workstation##, log in as Contoso99\Administrator. Click Start, All Programs, Microsoft Office, and then click Microsoft Office Outlook 2007.

31. Click Start, All Programs, Microsoft Office, and then click Microsoft Office Outlook 2007.

32. Under Mailbox—Administrator, highlight Calendar and click New to create a new calendar appointment.

33. Click Invite Attendees. Next, click the To button, select the Project-Managers group, and click Required. Select SmartBoard, click Resources, and click OK.

34. Type **Policies and Procedures Meeting** in the Subject dialog box.

35. Click Rooms next to the Location dialog box, select ConferenceRoom4, click Rooms, and click OK.

36. Select a Start and End time from 3:00 p.m. to 4:00 p.m. tomorrow and click Send.

37. Select tomorrow's date in the Calendar and view your appointment to see if there are any resource conflicts.

38. Close Outlook 2007 and close the Windows 7 machine.

Exercise 8-1-8   Moving Mailboxes

Overview	All the mailboxes you have created in this Lab have been stored within the Mailbox Database on the First Storage Group on NT2670Srv##A. To provide for fault tolerance, you plan to move mailboxes to other mailbox databases to balance the distribution of mailboxes in your organization.
	To complete this lab exercise, NT2670Srv##A and NT2670Srv##B must be started and have network access.
Completion time	15 minutes

1. On NT2670Srv##A, in the console tree pane of the Exchange Management Console, expand Recipient Configuration and highlight Mailbox.

2. While holding down the Ctrl key on your keyboard, select Meg Roombas, Jacques Guillere, Juan Ton, Sarah Parkers, Lois Lipshitz, Jessica Augustus, and Tom Hurt in the result pane.

3. Click Move Mailbox in the action pane.

4. At the Move Mailbox window, click Browse, select the Second Mailbox Database in the Third Storage Group on NT2670Srv##B, and click OK.

5. Click Next. Ensure that Skip the mailbox is selected and click Next.

6. Ensure that Immediately is selected and click Next. Click Move.

7. Once the move operation has completed, click Finish to close the Move Mailbox window.

8. While holding down the Ctrl key on your keyboard, select Bernadette Jones, Jennifer Coupland, Lisa Lackner, Mathew Kropf, Matt Adams, and David Schwan in the result pane.

9. Click Move Mailbox in the action pane.

10. At the Move Mailbox window, click Browse, select the Mailbox Database in the First Storage Group on NT2670Srv##B, and click OK.

11. Click Next. Ensure that Skip the mailbox is selected and click Next.

12. Ensure that Immediately is selected and click Next. Click Move.

13. Once the move operation has completed, click Finish to close the Move Mailbox window.

14. While holding down the Ctrl key on your keyboard, select SmartBoard, ConferenceRoom1, ConferenceRoom2, ConferenceRoom3, ConferenceRoom4, and ConferenceRoom5 in the result pane.

15. Click Move Mailbox in the action pane.

16. At the Move Mailbox window, click Browse, select the Second Mailbox Database in the Third Storage Group on NT2670Srv##B, and click OK.

17. Click Next. Ensure that Skip the mailbox is selected and click Next.

18. Ensure that Immediately is selected and click Next. Click Move.

19. Once the move operation has completed, click Finish to close the Move Mailbox window.

20. In the detail pane, click Create Filter.

21. Select Database and Equals from the two drop-down boxes. Click Browse, select the Mailbox Database in the First Storage Group, and click OK.

22. Click Apply Filter in the detail pane.

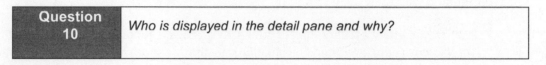

Question 10	Who is displayed in the detail pane and why?

23. Click Remove Filter in the detail pane.

24. Using the procedure outlined in Steps 20 to 23, view the mailboxes in all other mailbox databases to verify that your move operations were successful.

LAB REVIEW: QUESTIONS

Completion time   20 minutes

1. Describe what you learned by completing this lab.

2. Give some other examples of when you would need to add an additional email address to a mailbox user.

3. Why should you minimize the use of Full access mailbox permission?

4. In an organization, whom do you typically assign the Send on behalf and Send as mailbox permissions to?

5. When would you create a mail-enabled dynamic distribution group instead of a mail-enabled universal group?

6.   Explain how resource mailboxes reduce the administrative burden in your organization.

7.   If a user leaves your organization and their job role is assumed by an existing user, would you disconnect the existing user's mailbox? Explain.

LAB CHALLENGE: CONFIGURING RECIPIENTS USING THE EXCHANGE MANAGEMENT SHELL

Completion time	25 minutes

Although you have configured recipient objects using the Exchange Management Console in Exercises 8-1-1 through 8-1-8, you can also perform recipient configuration using cmdlets within the Exchange Management Shell.

Use the Exchange Management Shell to perform the following additional recipient configuration tasks:

- Create a new mailbox user for John Kerr (alias = john.kerr) in the Marketing OU of Contoso.com and store the mailbox in the Mailbox Database in the First Storage Group on NT2670Srv##A. Also ensure that John has an initial password of Secret123 and that the password must be changed at first logon.

- Ensure that John Kerr has a maximum send size of 5 MB.

- Create a new mail-enabled contact for Julie Bell (alias = julie.bell) in the Production OU of Contoso##.com that has an external email address of bellj@fizzure.net.

- Add Celine DeVries to the Project-Managers mail-enabled universal security group.

- Create a dynamic distribution group under the Contoso##.com domain that includes all mailbox users in the domain that are members of Project58.

- Move Meg Roombas' mailbox to the Mailbox Database in the First Storage Group on NT2670Srv##A. Ensure that the move operation fails if more than five corrupted messages are found.

LAB 8-2
USING THE MICROSOFT EXCHANGE BEST PRACTICES ANALYZER

This lab contains the following exercises:

Exercise 8-2-1 Running the Microsoft Exchange Best Practices Analyzer

Estimated lab time: 20 minutes

Exercise 8-2-1	Running the Microsoft Exchange Best Practices Analyzer
Overview	In this Lab Exercise, you will use the Microsoft Exchange Best Practices Analyzer too to help you tune the performance of your Exchange servers and detect configuration errors.
	To complete this lab exercise, NT2670Srv##A and NT2670Srv##B must be started and have network access.
Completion time	20 minutes

1. Turn on your NT2670Srv##A and NT2670Srv##B computers. On the NT2670Srv##A computer, when the logon screen appears, log on using your *Administrator* account and the password *P@ssw0rd*. If the Initial Configuration screen appears, close it.

2. Click Start, All Programs, Microsoft Exchange Server 2007, and then click Exchange Management Console.

3. In the console tree pane, click Toolbox.

4. In the action pane, double click Best Practices Analyzer.

5. At the Updates and Customer Feedback page, select Do not check for updates on startup and I don't want to join the program at this time, and click Go to Welcome screen.

6. At the Welcome to the Exchange Best Practices Analyzer page click Select options for a new scan.

7. At the Connect to Active Directory page ensure NT2670Srv##A is entered, and click Connect to Active Directory server.

8. At the Start a New Best Practices scan page, in the Enter an identifying label for this scan box enter ExchangeScan accept the defaults and click Start scanning.

9. When the scan is complete, at the Scanning Completed page click View a Report of this Best Practices scan.

Question 1	*What Critical Issues are displayed?*

Question 2	*What Report Types are available? Which view do you prefer?*

Question 3	*What other Exchange Best Practices Analyzer tests would you suggest performing?*

10. Close the Best Practices Analyzer.

11. Close the Exchange Management Console and log off of both computers.

LAB 9-1 70-236

CONFIGURING PUBLIC FOLDERS

This lab contains the following exercises:

Exercise 9-1-1 Configuring a Mail-Enabled Support Public Folder
Exercise 9-1-2 Creating Project Public Folders
Exercise 9-1-3 Configuring Public Folder Replicas
Lab Review: Questions
Lab Challenge: Configuring a Form for Public Folder Posts

Estimated lab time: 95 minutes

BEFORE YOU BEGIN

Lab 9-1 assumes that setup has been completed as specified in the setup document and that NT2670Srv##A and NT2670Srv##B have connectivity to the classroom network and the Internet. Moreover, Lab 9-1 assumes that you have completed the exercises in previous Labs.

NOTE	In this lab, you will see the characters ##. When you see these characters, substitute the two-digit number assigned to your computer.

SCENARIO

To help centralize IT support and provide information sharing for Project45 users, you will implement the appropriate public folders on NT2670Srv##A and configure content replicas on NT2670Srv##B.

In the Lab Challenge, you will configure the public folder to use a custom form.

After completing this lab, you will be able to:

- Create and mail enable public folders

- Configure public folder permissions and features

- Configure moderated public folders

- Configure public folders using bulk management commands

- Configure public folder content replicas

	Configuring a Mail-Enabled Support Public **Exercise 9-1-1 Folder**	
Overview	To simplify providing administrative support, you plan to create a Support mail-enabled public folder that MAPI clients can post items to or email when they need help. This folder should allow all internal and external users to post items but only allow Administrator to view and manage them. In addition, to alert Administrator of new entries, you should configure Administrator as the moderator for the Support public folder. You also wish to hide the mail-enabled public folder from Exchange address lists to prevent unnecessary emails. To complete this lab exercise, NT2670Srv##A, NT2670Srv##B and Workstation## must be started and have network access.	
Completion time	20 minutes	

NOTE

Make sure that the Microsoft Exchange Information Store and the Microsoft Exchange Mailbox Assistants services are running under Server Manager > Configuration > Services.

1. Turn on your NT2670Srv##A and NT2670Srv##B computers. On the NT2670Srv##A computer, when the logon screen appears, log on using your *Administrator* account and the password *P@ssw0rd*. If the Initial Configuration screen appears, close it.

2. Click Start, All Programs, Microsoft Exchange Server 2007, and then click Exchange Management Console.

3. In the console tree pane, highlight Toolbox and double click Public Folder Management Console in the detail pane.

4. Expand Default Public Folders in the console tree pane and highlight Default Public Folders.

> **NOTE** *Make sure that the Microsoft Exchange Information Store and the Microsoft Exchange Mailbox Assistants services are running under Server Manager > Configuration > Services.*

5. In the action pane, click New Public Folder.

6. At the New Public Folder window, type **Support** in the Name dialog box and click New.

7. Click Finish to close the New Mailbox window.

8. Expand Default Public Folders in the console tree pane and highlight Support in the detail pane.

9. In the action pane, click Mail Enable.

> **NOTE** *If you receive an error "The Active Directory Proxy object ..." you will need to reboot and make sure the Microsoft Exchange Information Store and Microsoft Exchange Mailbox Assistants are running.*

10. In the action pane, click Properties.

11. Highlight the Exchange General tab and select **Hide from Exchange address list**. Next, highlight the E-Mail Addresses tab and view the default email address.

> **Question 1** *What is the default alias and email address used for your public folder?*

12. Click OK to close public folder properties.

13. In the action pane, click Manage Send As Permission.

14. At the Manage Send As Permission window click Add, select Administrator, and click OK.

15. Click Manage.

16. Click Finish and close the Public Folder Management Console and the Exchange Management Console.

17. Turn on Workstation##, log in as Contoso99\Administrator. Click Start, All Programs, Microsoft Office, and then click Microsoft Office Outlook 2007.

18. Under Public Folders in the left pane, expand All Public Folders, right click Support, and click Properties.

NOTE	*You may have to click the Folder List icon (or Ctrl + 6) to see Public Folders.*

19. Highlight the Permissions tab of public folder properties. In the dialog box, highlight Default and select Contributor from the Permission Level drop-down dialog box.

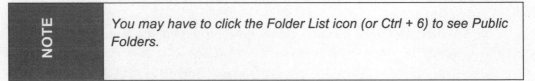

Question 2	*What type of access do internal and external senders have to the Support public folder?*
Question 3	*What type of access does Administrator have to the Support public folder?*

20. Highlight the Administration tab and click the Moderated Folder button.

NOTE	*Depending on the version of outlook you are using there may not be an Administration tab, if not click ok to close the Support public folder properties windows and skip to the next exercise.*

21. At the Moderated Folder window, select **Set folder up as a moderated folder**. Next, click To, select Administrator and click OK.

22. Select **Reply to new items**. Next, select Custom Response and click Template. When Outlook opens, type **IT Department Request Received** in the Subject dialog box and type **Thank you for your submission. You should receive a reply shortly regarding your problem. Be aware that it may take additional time to receive a response during times of high volume** in the body of the email.

23. Close the Outlook window and click Yes when prompted to save changes.

24. Next to the Moderators dialog box, click Add, select Administrator, and click OK.

25. Click OK to close the Moderated Folder window.

26. Click OK to close public folder properties.

27. Highlight Inbox under Mailbox—Tiger Smith in the left pane. Compose a new email from Tiger Smith to support@Contoso##.com. Observe the moderated folder autoreply that you receive.

28. Highlight Inbox under Mailbox—Administrator. View the email from Tiger Smith. Drag the email to the Support public folder for later use.

Exercise 9-1-2	Creating Project Public Folders
Overview	The mailbox users that are members of Project45 must use public folders to coordinate and distribute journals and meeting notes as well as post project comments. Project45 members should be able to post and manage their own journal items as well as post and view their own meeting notes, but should only be allowed to post comments. Mel Booker is in charge of the public folder hierarchy and should be given the necessary permissions to administer it as well as post, view, and manage all items within the public folders.
	To satisfy these requirements, you plan to implement a public folder hierarchy for them with the necessary permissions for each user. To simplify permission assignments, you will use bulk management commands within the Exchange Management Shell.
	To complete this lab exercise, NT2670Srv##A, NT2670Srv##B and Workstation## must be started and have network access.
Completion time	30 minutes

1. On Workstation##, in the Microsoft Outlook click on the Folder List icon in the lower left pane. In the Folder List window, expand Public Folders, All Public Folders.

2. Right click All Public Folders and select New Folder.

3. At the Create New Folder window, type **Project45** in the Name dialog box. Select Mail and Post Items in the drop-down box and click OK.

4. Right click Project45 and select New Folder.

5. At the Create New Folder window, type **Journals** in the Name dialog box. Select Journal Items in the drop-down box and click OK.

6. Right click Project45 and select New Folder.

7. At the Create New Folder window, type **Comments** in the Name dialog box. Select Mail and Post Items in the drop-down box and click OK.

8. Right click Project45 and select New Folder.

9. At the Create New Folder window, type **Meeting Notes** in the Name dialog box. Select Mail and Post Items in the drop-down box and click OK.

10. Close Microsoft Outlook.

11. On NT2670Srv##A, click Start, All Programs, Accessories, and then click Notepad.

12. Enter the following lines in Notepad:

    Identity

    "Tiger Smith"

    "Jacques Guillere"

    "Juan Ton"

    "Sarah Parkers"

    "Lois Lipshitz"

    "Jennifer Coupland"

    "Lisa Lackner"

    "Matthew Kropf"

13. Click File and then click Save. Type **"C:\Project45Members.csv"** in the File name dialog box **(you must use the double quotes)** and click Save.

14. Close Notepad.

15. Click Start, All Programs, Microsoft Exchange Server 2007, and then click Exchange Management Shell.

16. At the Exchange Management Shell prompt, type **Import-CSV "C:\Project45Members.csv" | ForEach-Object –Process { Add-PublicFolderClientPermission –Identity "\Project45" –Server "NT2670Srv##A" – User $_.Identity –AccessRights "Reviewer" }** and press Enter.

NOTE	*If you get an error stating that the specified public folder user "user name" does not exist. ... You will need to enable the mailbox for each account identified in step 12.*

Question 4	*What type of access does the Reviewer client permission grant to Project45 users for the Project45 public folder?*

17. At the Exchange Management Shell prompt, type **Import-CSV "C:\Project45Members.csv" | ForEach-Object –Process { Add-PublicFolderClientPermission –Identity "\Project45\Comments" –Server "NT2670Srv##A" –User $_.Identity –AccessRights "NonEditingAuthor" }** and press Enter.

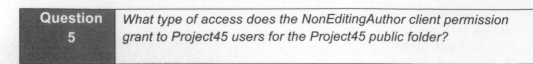

Question 5 — *What type of access does the NonEditingAuthor client permission grant to Project45 users for the Project45 public folder?*

18. At the Exchange Management Shell prompt, type **Import-CSV "C:\Project45Members.csv" | ForEach-Object –Process { Add-PublicFolderClientPermission –Identity "\Project45\Journals" –Server "NT2670Srv##A" –User $_.Identity –AccessRights "Author" }** and press Enter.

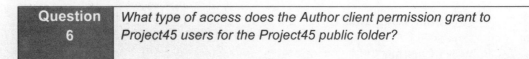

Question 6 — *What type of access does the Author client permission grant to Project45 users for the Project45 public folder?*

19. At the Exchange Management Shell prompt, type **Import-CSV "C:\Project45Members.csv" | ForEach-Object –Process { Add-PublicFolderClientPermission –Identity "\Project45\Meeting Notes" –Server "NT2670Srv##A" –User $_.Identity –AccessRights "Contributor" }** and press Enter.

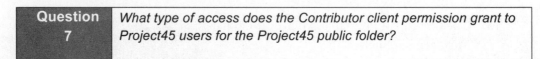

Question 7 — *What type of access does the Contributor client permission grant to Project45 users for the Project45 public folder?*

20. Click Start, All Programs, Accessories, and then click Notepad.

21. Enter the following lines in Notepad:

    Folder
    "\Project45"
    "\Project45\Journals"
    "\Project45\Meeting Notes"
    "\Project45\Comments"

22. Click File and then click Save. Type **"C:\Project45Folders.csv"** in the File name dialog box **(you must use the double quotes)** and click Save.

23. Close Notepad.

24. Click Start, All Programs, Microsoft Exchange Server 2007, and then click Exchange Management Shell.

25. At the Exchange Management Shell prompt, type **Import-CSV "C:\Project45Folders.csv" | ForEach-Object –Process { Add-PublicFolderClientPermission –Identity $_.Folder –Server "NT2670Srv##A" –User "Mel Booker" –AccessRights "Editor" }** and press Enter.

Question 8	*What type of access does the Editor client permission grant to Mel Booker for the Project45 public folders?*

26. At the Exchange Management Shell prompt, type **Import-CSV "C:\Project45Folders.csv" | ForEach-Object –Process { Add-PublicFolderAdministrativePermission –Identity $_.Folder –Server "NT2670Srv##A" –User "Mel Booker" –AccessRights "AllExtendedRights" }** and press Enter.

Question 9	*What type of access does the All Extended Rights administrative permission grant to Mel Booker for the Project45 public folders?*

27. At the Exchange Management Shell prompt, type **Import-CSV "C:\Project45Folders.csv" | ForEach-Object –Process { Get-PublicFolderClientPermission –Identity $_.Folder –Server "NT2670Srv##A" | Format-List }** and press Enter. Verify your client public folder permission assignments.

28. At the Exchange Management Shell prompt, type **Import-CSV "C:\Project45Folders.csv" | ForEach-Object –Process { Get-PublicFolderAdministrativePermission –Identity $_.Folder –Server "NT2670Srv##A" | Format-List }** and press Enter. Verify your administrative public folder permission assignments.

29. Close the Exchange Management Shell.

Exercise 9-1-3   Configuring Public Folder Replicas

Overview	Some Project45 users complain that access to the Project45 public folders is quite slow. After investigation, you notice that these users are connecting to the public folder database on NT2670Srv##B and are redirected to the public folder database on NT2670Srv##A using public folder referrals.
	To allow Project45 users to access their public folders from either NT2670Srv##A or NT2670Srv##B, you plan to create a public folder replica on NT2670Srv##B that holds the Project45 folders that you created on NT2670Srv## after working hours (8:00 a.m. to 6:00 p.m.). Moreover, to reduce the strain on public folder replication, you plan to configure the Project45 public folders to remove any items older than 14 days because Project45 items are no longer needed after two weeks.
	To complete this lab exercise, NT2670Srv##A and NT2670Srv##B must be started and have network access.
Completion time	10 minutes

1. On NT2670Srv##A, click Start, All Programs, Microsoft Exchange Server 2007, and then click Exchange Management Console.

2. In the console tree pane, highlight Tools and double click Public Folder Management Console in the detail pane.

3. Expand Default Public Folders in the console tree pane, highlight the Project45 public folder in the detail pane and click Properties in the action pane.

4. Highlight the Replication tab and click Add. Select the Public Folder Database on NT2670Srv##B and click OK.

5. Deselect **Use public folder database replication schedule** and click Customize. Highlight the cells that represent 8:00 a.m. to 6:00 p.m. Monday to Friday and click OK.

6. Type **14** in the **Local replica age limit** dialog box and highlight the Limits tab.

7. Deselect Use database age defaults and type **14** in the **Age limit for replicas (days)** dialog box.

8. Click OK.

9. Using the procedure outlined in Steps 3 to 8, ensure that the Comments, Journals, and Meeting Notes folders under the Project45 public folder are also replicated to the public folder database on NT2670Srv##B using the same schedule and restrictions.

10. Close the Public Folder Management Console and close the Exchange Management Console and log off all machines.

LAB REVIEW: QUESTIONS

Completion time   15 minutes

1. Describe what you learned by completing this lab.

2. What is another way to configure your Exchange organization so that emails sent to support@NT2670Srv##A.com are sent to Administrator?

3. Explain why you could not use the Public Folder Management Console to create the Journal public folder in Exercise 9-1-2.

4. What is the difference between the **Local replica age limit** and **Age limit for replicas** settings in Exercise 9-1-3?

LAB CHALLENGE: CONFIGURING A FORM FOR PUBLIC FOLDER POSTS

Completion time   20 minutes

Project45 users post comments regularly to the Project45\Comments public folder. To standardize the information that is included within the Project45\Comments public folder, you wish to create a custom form that includes fields to identify the nature of the comment as well as the area of Project45 that it applies to.

Create a new custom form based on a standard post item that satisfies these requirements and ensure that new post items in the Project45\Comments public folder use this form by default. When finished create a new post in the Project45\Comments public folder to test your configuration.

LAB 9-2 70-236
CONFIGURING PROTOCOLS AND TRANSPORT RULES

This lab contains the following exercises:

Exercise 9-2-1 Configuring POP3 and IMAP4
Exercise 9-2-2 Configuring HTTP
Exercise 9-2-3 Configuring SMTP
Exercise 9-2-4 Configuring a Transport Rule
Lab Review: Questions
Lab Challenge: Configuring Additional Transport Rules

Estimated lab time: 105 minutes

BEFORE YOU BEGIN

Lab 9-2 assumes that setup has been completed as specified in the setup document and that NT2670Srv##A and NT2670Srv##B have connectivity to the classroom network and the Internet. Moreover, Lab 9-2 assumes that you have completed the exercises in previous Tasks.

NOTE	*In this lab, you will see the characters ##. When you see these characters, substitute the two-digit number assigned to your computer.*

SCENARIO

Now that you have configured the appropriate recipient objects and policies, you need to ensure that the client access protocols on your CAS role servers are correctly configured to allow for client access within your organization as well as configure client access protocol restrictions. In addition, you will need to configure a transport rule on your Hub role server to alter the processing of email to match company needs.

In the Lab Challenge, you will configure additional transport rules on the Hub and Edge role servers within your organization.

After completing this lab, you will be able to:

- Configure the POP3, IMAP4, HTTP, and Outlook Anywhere protocols on a CAS role server

- Configure the SMTP protocol on a Hub role server

- Configure transport rules on Hub and Edge role servers

Exercise 9-2-1	Configuring POP3 and IMAP4
Overview	Although your organization allows both POP3 and IMAP4 connections for email retrieval from outside the organization, POP3 is only used by a small number of older email clients and some wireless portable devices that do not support TLS and rich text formats. IMAP4 is the recommended protocol for accessing email outside of the organization and is used by many organization members from their email clients at home.
	As a result, you plan to configure your POP3 and IMAP4 services accordingly. In addition, you plan to limit the number of POP3 connections to 50 and the number of IMAP4 connections to 500 for each CAS role server to reflect the number of POP3 and IMAP4 clients that you expect to have in the next year.
	To complete this lab exercise, NT2670Srv##A and NT2670Srv##B must be started and have network access.
Completion time	15 minutes

1. Turn on your NT2670Srv##A and NT2670Srv##B computers. On the NT2670Srv##A computer, when the logon screen appears, log on using your *Administrator* account and the password *P@ssw0rd*. If the Initial Configuration screen appears, close it.

2. Click Start, All Programs, Microsoft Exchange Server 2007, and then click Exchange Management Console.

3. In the console tree pane, expand Server Configuration and select Client Access.

4. Select NT2670Srv##A in the detail pane and highlight the POP3 and IMAP4 tabs in the work pane.

5. In the work pane, highlight POP3 and click Properties in the action pane.

 If the binding tab is not visible, close the properties window and double click POP3 in the work pane.

6. Highlight the Binding tab.

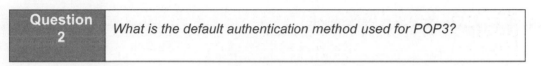 *What are the default ports used for POP3, POP3+TLS, and POP3+SSL?*

7. Highlight the Authentication tab.

Question 2	*What is the default authentication method used for POP3?*

8. Select **Plain text logon**.

9. Highlight the Connection tab and enter **50** in the **Maximum connections** and **Maximum connections from a single IP address** dialog boxes.

10. Click OK.

11. Click in the work pane, highlight IMAP4, and click Properties in the action pane.

 If the binding tab is not visible, close the properties window and double click IMPA4 in the work pane.

12. Highlight the Binding tab.

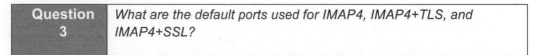 *What are the default ports used for IMAP4, IMAP4+TLS, and IMAP4+SSL?*

13. Highlight the Authentication tab and note the default authentication method of TLS.

14. Highlight the Connection tab and enter **500** in the **Maximum connections** and **Maximum connections from a single IP address** dialog boxes.

15. Click OK.

16. Using the procedure outlined in Steps 4 through 15, configure the POP3 and IMAP4 protocols on NT2670Srv##B.

> **NOTE**
>
> *You may need to start the Microsoft Exchange Information Store and the Microsoft Exchange Mailbox Assistants services on NT2670Srv##B using the Services console.*

17. Click Start, All Programs, Administrative Tools, and then click Services.

18. Right click Microsoft Exchange POP3 and click Restart.

19. Right click Microsoft Exchange IMAP4 and click Restart.

20. Close the Services console.

21. On NT2670Srv##B, log in as Administrator.

22. Using the procedure outlined in Steps 17 through 20, restart the POP3 and IMAP4 services on NT2670Srv##B.

Exercise 9-2-2	Configuring HTTP
Overview	Your organization also allows the use of OWA for access email internally and externally when other methods are unavailable. However, by default, OWA forces users to type Contoso##.com\username at the OWA logon screen.
	You must ensure that OWA is configured to allow for internal and external access for up to 200 concurrent connections per CAS role server as well as ensure that users only need to type their username at the OWA logon screen (their domain name should be automatically supplied).
	To complete this lab exercise, NT2670Srv##A and NT2670Srv##B must be started and have network access.
Completion time	15 minutes

1. On NT2670Srv##A, in the console tree pane of the Exchange Management Console, expand Server Configuration and select Client Access.

2. Select NT2670Srv##A in the detail pane and highlight the Outlook Web Access tab in the work pane.

3. Highlight owa (Default Web Site) in the work pane and click Properties in the action pane.

4. Ensure that **https://NT2670Srv##A.Contoso##.com** is entered in the Internal URL and External URL dialog boxes to provide for internal and external access to OWA.

5. Highlight the Authentication tab and ensure that **Use form-based authentication** is selected. Next, select User name only, click the Browse button, select Contoso##.com, and click OK. Close the warning box.

6. Click OK to close owa (Default Webs Site) properties.

7. Using the procedure outlined in Steps 2 to 6, configure NT2670Srv##B to use the URL **https://NT2670Srv##B.Contoso##.com** for internal and external requests as well as ensure that users only need to type their username in the OWA logon box.

Question 4	What must happen before the OWA changes that you made take effect?

8. Click Start, All Programs, Administrative Tools, and then click Internet Information Services (IIS) Manager.

9. At the Internet Information Services (IIS) Manager window, expand NT2670Srv##A, Sites in the left pane.

10. Click Default Web Site and click Limits… under the Configure heading of the Action pane.

11. Select **Limit number of connections:**, and enter **200** in the dialog box.

12. Click OK to close the Edit Web Site Limits dialog box.

13. Click NT2670Srv##A in the left pane, click Restart under the Manage Server heading in the Actions pane.

14. Close the Internet Information Services (IIS) Manager console.

15. On NT2670Srv##B, log in as Administrator.

16. Using the procedure outlined in Steps 8 to 14, configure the Default Web Site on NT2670Srv##B to allow a maximum of 200 concurrent connections and restart IIS on NT2670Srv##B.

Exercise 9-2-3	Configuring SMTP
Overview	To allow for SMTP relay from the POP3 and IMAP4 clients within your organization, you have implemented the appropriate send and receive connectors in Lab 6, Task 3. Because NT2670Srv##A hosts four server roles (Mailbox, Hub, CAS, and UM), you would like to ensure that SMTP relay does not exceed 500 concurrent outbound connections on the server.

Additionally, you must also prevent out-of-office replies, delivery reports, and nondelivery reports to all external domains. However, one of your partner organizations, Initech Inc. (initech.com), requires out-of-office replies, delivery reports, and nondelivery reports. Moreover, any emails sent to Initech must not use Exchange rich-text format.

To complete this lab exercise, NT2670Srv##A and NT2670Srv##B must be started and have network access. |
| Completion time | 10 minutes |

1. On NT2670Srv##A, in the console tree pane of the Exchange Management Console, expand Server Configuration and highlight Hub Transport.

2. Highlight NT2670Srv##A in the detail pane and click Properties in the action pane.

3. Highlight the Limits tab, enter **500** in the **Maximum concurrent outbound connections** dialog box and click OK.

   NOTE: if the Limits tab does not display, close the properties window and double click on NT2670Srv##A and then click on the Limits tab.

4. In the console tree pane, expand Organization Configuration and highlight Hub Transport.

5. Highlight the Remote Domains tab in the detail pane, select Default in the work pane, and click Properties from the action pane.

6. On the General tab of the Default remote domain properties, click **Allow none**.

7. Highlight the **Format of original message sent as attachment to journal report** tab, deselect **Allow non-delivery reports** and **Allow delivery reports**, and click OK.

8. In the action pane, click New Remote Domain.

9. At the New Remote Domain window, type **Initech** in the Name dialog box and type **initech.com** in the Domain name dialog box. Next, select **Include all subdomains** and click New.

10. Click Finish to close the New Remote Domain window.

11. Select Initech in the work pane and click Properties from the action pane.

12. Click **Allow external out-of-office messages and out-of-office messages sent by Outlook 2003 or earlier clients or sent by Exchange Server 2003 or earlier servers**.

13. Highlight the **Format of original message sent as attachment to journal report** tab, select **Never use** in the Exchange rich-text format section, and click OK.

Exercise 9-2-4	Configuring a Transport Rule
Overview	For legal purposes, external communication regarding Project45 and Project58 should be minimized within your organization. Any emails sent to external recipients regarding Project45 and Project58 should contain a legal disclaimer that identifies the confidential nature of the information included within. This legal disclaimer should be appended to the email with a separator line using a medium-size blue font. In addition, a copy of these external project emails must be sent to Administrator for auditing purposes.
	To comply with these requirements, you plan to create a transport rule on the Hub role servers within your organization.
	To complete this lab exercise, NT2670Srv## and NT2670Srv##B must be started and have network access.
Completion time	20 minutes

1. On NT2670Srv##A, in the console tree pane of the Exchange Management Console, expand Organization Configuration and highlight Hub Transport.

2. In the action pane, click New Transport Rule.

3. At the New Transport Rule window, type **External Project Emails** in the Name dialog box, and type **This transport rule appends a legal disclaimer to all external Project45 and Project58 emails as well as sends a copy of these emails to Administrator for auditing** in the Comment dialog box.

4. Verify that Enable Rule is selected to ensure that the transport rule is enabled after creation and click Next.

5. In the **Step 1: Select condition(s)** section, select **sent to users inside or outside the organization**.

6. In the **Step 2: Edit the rule description by clicking an underlined value** click the **Inside** underlined word. In the Select scope window that appears, select Outside from the drop-down box and click OK.

7. In the **Step 1: Select condition(s)** section, select **when the Subject field or the body of the message contains specific words**.

8. In the **Step 2: Edit the rule description by clicking an underlined value** section, click the **specific words** underlined words. In the Specify words window that appears, type **Project45** and click Add. Next, type **Project58**, click Add, and click OK.

9. Click Next.

10. In the **Step 1: Select action(s)** section on the Actions page, select append disclaimer text using font, size, color, with separator, and fallback to action if unable to apply.

Question 5	*What is the default configuration of the disclaimer text shown in the* ***Step 2: Edit the rule description by clicking an underlined value*** *dialog box?*

11. In the **Step 2: Edit the rule description by clicking an underlined value** section, click the **disclaimer text** underlined words. In the Select disclaimer text window that appears, type the following text in the Disclaimer text dialog box and click OK.

    This transmission (including any attachments) may contain confidential information, privileged material (including material protected by the solicitor-client or other applicable privileges), or constitute nonpublic information. Any use of this information by anyone other than the intended recipient is prohibited. If you have received this transmission in error, please immediately reply to the sender and delete this information from your system. Use, dissemination, distribution, or reproduction of this transmission by unintended recipients is not authorized and may be unlawful.

12. Click the **smallest** underlined word. In the Select font size window that appears, select Normal from the drop-down box and click OK.

13. Click the **Gray** underlined word. In the Select font color window that appears, select Blue from the drop-down box and click OK.

14. In the **Step 1: Select action(s)** section of the Actions page, select **Blind carbon copy (Bcc) the message to addresses**.

15. In the **Step 2: Edit the rule description by clicking an underlined value** section, click the **addresses** underlined word. In the Select recipients text window that appears, click Add, select Administrator, and click OK.

16. Click OK again to return to the Actions page and click Next.

17. At the Exceptions page, click Next.

18. At the Create Rule page, click New.

19. Click Finish to close the New Transport Rule window.

20. Close the Exchange Management Console.

21. Turn on Workstation##, log in as Contoso99\Administrator. Click Start, All Programs, Microsoft Office, and then click Microsoft Office Outlook 2007.

22. In the left pane of Outlook 2007, expand Mailbox—Tiger Smith and highlight Inbox.

 You will need to create an account for Tiger Smith in Outlook 2007 before you can perform the next few steps.

23. Click New to compose a new email.

24. Click the From button and select Tiger Smith.

25. In the To field, type **someperson@somedomain.com**. Type **Transport Rule Test** in the Subject field. Type **Project45 information** in the body and click the Send button.

26. Expand Mailbox—Administrator in the left pane of Outlook 2007 and highlight Inbox. Double click the related email from Tiger Smith to verify that your transport rule was applied.

27. Close the email and Outlook 2007.

LAB REVIEW QUESTIONS

Completion time   15 minutes

1. Describe what you learned by completing this lab.

2. Explain why it is important to limit the number of concurrent client connections on your CAS role servers.

3. Why is it important to configure remote domains on your Hub role servers?

4. Why did you not need to configure the transport rule on NT2670Srv##B in Exercise 9-2-4?

LAB CHALLENGE: CONFIGURING ADDITIONAL TRANSPORT RULES

Completion time	30 minutes

In addition to the transport rule that you have configured in Exercise 9-2-4, configure an additional transport rule on your Hub role servers that sends a copy of all messages to Administrator that are marked with the "Extremely Confidential" custom message classification. You must first ensure that custom message classification is created. In addition, you must add the custom message classification to your Outlook 2007 client on NT2670Srv##A and test your configuration.

Following this, create a transport rule on your Edge role server that automatically deletes any emails with a Spam Confidence Level (SCL) of eight or greater.

LAB 10-1 70-236
CONFIGURING SECURITY

This lab contains the following exercises:

Exercise 10-1-1 Reducing the Edge Role Attack Surface
Exercise 10-1-2 Configuring Forefront Security for Exchange
Exercise 10-1-3 Configuring CA-Signed Certificates for Protocol Encryption
Exercise 10-1-4 Implementing User Certificates
Exercise 10-1-5 Defragmenting and Repairing Exchange Databases
Lab Review: Questions
Lab Challenge: Configuring a Block List Provider

Estimated lab time: 115 minutes

BEFORE YOU BEGIN

Lab 10-1 assumes that setup has been completed as specified in the setup document and that NT2670Srv##A and NT2670Srv##B have connectivity to the classroom network and the Internet. Moreover, Lab 10-1 assumes that you have completed the exercises in previous Labs.

> NOTE
>
> *Microsoft Exchange Information Server, Microsoft Exchange Assistants, and DNS are critical services for this lab. If you are experiencing problems make sure that these three services are started on both NT2670Srv##A and NT2670Srv##B servers.*

> NOTE
>
> *In this lab, you will see the characters ##. When you see these characters, substitute the two-digit number assigned to your computer.*

SCENARIO

To provide security for your Exchange infrastructure, you will need to configure the appropriate technologies. For your Edge role server, you plan to use the Security Configuration Wizard (SCW) to stop unnecessary services and implement Windows Firewall. In addition, you plan to configure antispam agents on your Edge role server to reduce incoming Internet spam as well as install and configure Forefront Security for Exchange (FSE) to minimize viruses that are sent to your organization.

To provide better security on the other Exchange servers within your organization, you plan to replace the default self-signed certificates used for SSL and TLS with CA-signed certificates from an Enterprise CA. Moreover, this Enterprise CA will also be used to sign user certificates used for email encryption and signing.

In the Lab Challenge, you will configure a block list provider on your Edge role server.

After completing this lab, you will be able to:

- Use the SCW to configure services and firewall settings

- Configure the antispam agents on an Edge role server

- Install and configure Forefront Security for Exchange

- Install and configure an Enterprise CA

- Configure CA-signed certificates for use by IMAP4, POP3, UM, HTTP, and SMTP

- Deploy and configure user certificates for email encryption and signing

Exercise 10-1-1   Reducing the Edge Role Attack Surface

Overview	You wish to reduce its attack surface by disabling unnecessary services and restricting access to ports using Windows Firewall on NT2670Srv##B. To identify and configure the appropriate settings, you plan to use the Security Configuration Wizard (SCW) component of Windows.
	To complete this lab exercise, NT2670Srv##B must be started and have network access.
Completion time	20 minutes

1. Turn on your NT2670Srv##A and NT2670Srv##B computers. On the NT2670Srv##B computer, when the logon screen appears, log on using your *Administrator* account and the password *P@ssw0rd*. If the Initial Configuration screen appears, close it.

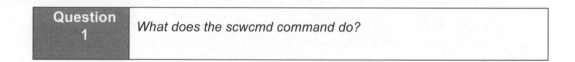

Question 1	*What does the scwcmd command do?*

2. On the NT2670Srv##B computer click Start, Administrative Tools, and then click Security Configuration Wizard. When the Security Configuration Wizard window appears, click Next.

3. At the Configuration Action screen ensure that **Create a new security policy** is selected and click Next.

4. At the Select Server screen, click Browse, select NT2670Srv##B, and click OK.

5. When finished, click Next.

6. After a few moments, click View Configuration Database to open the SCW Viewer window. View the information regarding Edge role services, close the SCW Viewer, and click Next.

NOTE	*Click Yes if you get a message window "An ActiveX control on this page might be unsafe ..."*

7. At the Role-Based Service Configuration page, click Next.

8. At the Select Server Roles page, deselect **File Server** and click Next.

9. At the Select Client Features page, deselect **DHCP client (if it is an option)** and click Next.

10. At the Select Administration and Other Options page, click Next.

11. At the Additional Services page, click Next.

12. At the Handling Unspecified Services page, ensure that **Do not change the startup mode of the service** is selected and click Next.

13. At the Confirm Service Changes window, review the proposed changes to the existing services on your computer and click Next.

14. At the Network Security Configuration page, click Next.

15. At the Network Security Rules page, review the open ports and click Next.

16. At the Registry Settings page select Skip this section and click Next.

17. At the Audit Policy page select Skip this section and click Next.

18. At the Save Security Policy page, click Next.

19. At the Security Policy File Name page, type **C:\SCW-Edge.xml** in the Security policy file name dialog box and click Next.

Question 2	What can the C:\SCW-Edge.xml file be used for?

20. Click OK to close the information window.

21. Select Apply now and click Next.

22. Click Next and then click Finish to close the Security Configuration Wizard.

23. Reboot NT2670Srv##B.

Exercise 10-1-2   Configuring Forefront Security for Exchange

Overview	To provide for virus detection for inbound email from the Internet, you have decided to install and configure Forefront Security for Exchange (FSE) on server (NT2670Srv##B).
	To complete this lab exercise, NT2670Srv##B must be started and have network access. In addition you must first download a 120-day evaluation copy of FSE from the Microsoft Web site.
Completion time	25 minutes

1. On NT2670Srv##B, log in as the local Administrator account.

2. Navigate to the folder that contains the FSE setup files and double click setup.exe. When the Welcome page appears, click Next.

3. On the License Agreement page, click Yes.

4. On the Customer Information page, enter your name and company in the appropriate dialog boxes and click Next.

5. On the Installation Location page, ensure that Local Installation is selected and click Next.

6. On the Installation Type page, ensure that Full Installation is selected and click Next.

7. At the Use Microsoft Update Page, select I don't want to use Microsoft Update and click Next.

8. At the Quarantine Security Settings page, click Next.

9. At the Engines page, select four more antivirus engines of your choice and click Next.

Question 3	Which engine is selected by default?

10. At the Proxy Server page, click Next.

11. At the Choose Destination Location page, click Next.

12. At the Select Program Folder page, click Next.

13. At the Start Copying Files page, click Next.

14. At the Restart Exchange Transport Service page, click Next to restart the Exchange Transport Service to activate Forefront.

If you get an error that the MicrosoftIS server could not start you will need to start the service on both NT2670Srv##A and NT2670Srv##B and reinstall FSE.

15. At the Recycling Exchange Transport Service page, click Next.

16. Click Finish to close the FSE setup window.

17. Reboot NT2670Srv##B, and log in using the Administrator account.

18. Click Start, All Programs, Microsoft Forefront Server Security, Exchange Server, and then click Forefront Server Security Administrator.

19. Ensure that NT2670Srv##B is entered into the What server do you want to connect to text box. Click Ok on the License Information page.

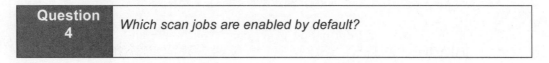
Question 4   *Which scan jobs are enabled by default?*

20. Under the Settings section in the left pane of FSE, select Antivirus.

21. Select **Max Certainty** in the Bias drop-down box.

22. Select **Delete: remove infection** in the Action drop-down box.

23. Under the Settings section in the left pane of FSE, select General Options (Click Yes when prompted to save your changes) and ensure that the **Scan on scanner update** option is selected.

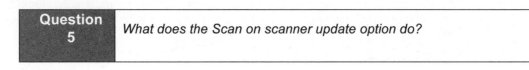
Question 5   *What does the Scan on scanner update option do?*

24. Under the Settings section in the left pane of FSE, select Scanner Updates (Click Yes when prompted to save your changes) and click Update Now.

25. Close Forefront Server Security Administrator.

Exercise 10-1-3	Configuring CA-Signed Certificates for Protocol Encryption
Overview	To enhance the security of your Exchange organization, you wish to replace the default self-signed certificate used for SSL and TLS connections with a CA-signed certificate.
	To achieve this, you plan to install a CA on NT2670Srv##A and issue the CA trusted root certificate to all domain computers. Next, you will use IIS Manager to remove the existing certificate and enroll for a CA-signed certificate for NT2670Srv##A and NT2670Srv##B. Finally, you must ensure that the CA-signed certificate is used for IMAP4, POP3, UM, HTTP, and SMTP.
	To complete this lab exercise, NT2670Srv##A and NT2670Srv##B must be started and have network access.
Completion time	60 minutes

1. On NT2670Srv##A, log in as Administrator, if the Server Manager console does not appear; click Start > Administrative Tools > Server Manager. In the Server Manager scope pane, select the Roles node, and then click Add Roles.

2. Click Next to bypass the *Before You Begin* page. The *Select Server Roles* page appears.

3. Select the Active Directory Certificate Services checkbox, and click Next. An Add Roles Wizard message box appears, listing the features required to add the Web Server (IIS) role.

4. At the Active Directory Certificate Services (AD CS) page, click Next.

5. At the Select Role Services page, select Certificate Authority and click Next.

6. At the Specify Setup Type page, select Enterprise and click Next.

7. At the Specify CA Type page, select Root CA and click Next.

8. At the Set Up Private Key page, select Create a new private key and click Next.

9. At the Configure Cryptography for CA page, click Next.

10. At the Configure CA Name page, click Next.

11. At the Set Validity Period page, click Next.

12. At the Configure Certificate Database page, click Next.

13. At the Confirm Installation Selections page, click Install.

14. Click Start, Administrative Tools, and then click Certification Authority.

15. Click Start, All Programs, Administrative Tools, and then click Internet Information Services (IIS) Manager.

16. At the Internet Information Services (IIS) Manager window, click NT2670Srv##A, and double click Server Certificates.

17. At the Server Certificates page in the Actions pane select Create Certificate Request.

18. At the Distinguished Name Properties page, in the common name text box, enter Contoso99.com. In the Organization text box, enter Contoso Inc. In the Organizational unit text box, enter Headquarters. In the City and State text boxes enter your City and State respectively and click Next.

19. At the Cryptographic Service Provider Properties, click Next.

20. At the File Name window enter contoso## and click Finish.

21. Click Default Web Site, at the Default Web Site Home page, lick SSL Settings. Ensure that **Require secure channel (SSL)** and **Require 128-bit encryption**.

22. Close the IIS Manager.

23. Click Start, All Programs, Microsoft Exchange Server 2007, and then click Exchange Management Shell.

24. At the Exchange Management Shell prompt, type **Get-ExchangeCertificate** and press Enter.

Question 6	What is the Subject name of the default self-signed certificate for NT2670Srv##A called?
Question 7	What is the Subject name of the CA-signed certificate for NT2670Srv##A called?
Question 8	Is the CA-signed certificate used for all of the available services and protocols (IPUWS in the Services column)?

25. Write down the thumbprint for the CA-signed certificate for NT2670Srv##A.

26. At the Exchange Management Shell prompt, type **Enable-ExchangeCertificate -Thumbprint** *thumbprint* **-Services "IMAP, POP, UM, IIS, SMTP"** and press Enter where *thumbprint* is the thumbprint that you recorded in the previous step.

27. At the Exchange Management Shell prompt, type **Get-ExchangeCertificate** and press Enter. Verify that the CA-signed certificate is configured for use with all protocols and services.

28. Close the Exchange Management Shell.

Exercise 10-1-4	Implementing User Certificates
Overview	Several users within your organization have requested email encryption within their Outlook clients. Before deploying user certificates to these users, you plan to test the configuration of user certificates using your own user account.
	To complete this lab exercise, NT2670Srv## and NT2670Srv##B must be started and have network access.
Completion time	10 minutes

1. Turn on Workstation##, log in as Contoso99\Administrator. Click Start and enter **certmgr.msc** and press Enter.

2. In the left pane of the Certificates—Current User window, right click Personal, select All Tasks, and click Request New Certificate.

3. At the Certificate Request Wizard window, click Next.

4. At the Select Certificate Enrollment policy page, click Next.

5. On the Request Certificates page, select User and click Enroll.

 If you receive an error that the server cannot be found make sure that DNS has been started on both NT2670Srv##A and NT2670Srv##B servers.

6. Click Finish to close the Certificate Request Wizard and view the user certificate listed in the right pane of the Certificate—Current User window.

Question 9	*Where is the user certificate stored?*

7. Close the Certificates—Current User window.

8. Click Start, All Programs, Microsoft Office, and then click Microsoft Office Outlook 2007.

9.   Click the Tools menu and select Trust Center.

Depending on your version of Outlook you are using, you may have to click on the File menu, then options to access the Trust Center. Then click Trust Center settings to configure the options below.

10.   At the Trust Center window, click E-mail Security in the left pane and select the **Encrypt contents and attachments for outgoing messages** and **Add digital signature to outgoing messages** options.

11.   Click Settings, ensure that the previously configured certificate is listed in the Signing Certificate (if not click Choose and select it) and Encryption Certificate dialog boxes and click OK.

Depending on your version of Outlook you are using, you may have to provide a name before saving security settings.

12.   Click OK to close the Trust Center window.

13.   Close the email and Outlook 2007.

Exercise 10-1-5	Defragmenting and Repairing Exchange Databases
Overview	Sometimes, database corruption can be prevented or repaired using the eseutil.exe or isinteg.exe utilities. In this exercise, you will inspect, defragment and repair a mailbox database using the eseutil.exe and isinteg.exe utilities. To complete this lab exercise, NT2670Srv##B must be started and have network access.
Completion time	10 minutes

1. On NT2670Srv##B, log in as Administrator.

2. Click Start, All Programs, Microsoft Exchange Server 2007, and then click Exchange Management Shell.

3. At the Exchange Management Shell prompt, type **Dismount-Database -Identity 'NT2670Srv##B\Third Storage Group\Second Mailbox Database'** and press Enter. Type Y and click enter when prompted to confirm this action.

4. Click Start, All Programs, Accessories, and click Command Prompt. At the Windows command prompt, type **eseutil.exe /g "C:\SG3\Second Mailbox Database.edb"** and press Enter.

Question 10	What does the /g option of eseutil.exe do?

5. At the Windows command prompt, type **eseutil.exe /d "C:\SG3\Second Mailbox Database.edb"** and press Enter.

Question 11	What does the /d option of eseutil.exe do?

6. At the Windows command prompt, type **eseutil.exe /p "C:\SG3\Second Mailbox Database.edb"** and press Enter. Read the warning and click Cancel.

Question 12	What does the /p option of eseutil.exe do and why is it not recommended for use on a database that is not damaged?

7. At the Windows command prompt, type **isinteg.exe –s NT2670Srv##B –fix –test alltests** and press Enter. Observe the menu that is displayed.

8. Type the number that corresponds to the Second Mailbox Database in the Third Storage Group (it should be marked as offline) and press Enter.

9. Type **y** and press Enter to perform the tests. Observe the results.

Question 13	What will happen if isinteg.exe detects errors and why?

10. Close the Windows command prompt.

11. Click Start, All Programs, Microsoft Exchange Server 2007, and then click Exchange Management Shell.

12. At the Exchange Management Shell prompt, type **Mount-Database -Identity 'NT2670Srv##B\Third Storage Group\Second Mailbox Database'** and press Enter.

13. Close the Exchange Management Shell.

LAB REVIEW: QUESTIONS

Completion time   15 minutes

1. Describe what you learned by completing this lab.

2. Why should you use the SCW to configure system service startup and Windows Firewall when both of these tasks can be performed using the Services Console and Network Properties?

3. Why is it a good practice to install at a minimum Forefront Security for Exchange on the Edge role servers within your organization?

4. Briefly explain why you should replace the default self-signed SSL/TLS certificate with a CA-signed certificate?

5. In Exercise 10-1-3, why did you need to configure the Default Domain Policy?

6. Explain the benefits and disadvantages of using a larger number of bits when generating a certificate.

7. In Exercise 10-1-4, what would happen if you tested the user certificate for Administrator in Outlook by sending a message from Administrator to Tiger Smith?

8. Why is the isinteg.exe utility better to use on a corrupted database than the /p option to the eseutil.exe utility?

LAB CHALLENGE: CONFIGURING A BLOCK LIST PROVIDER

Completion time   15 minutes

Using the Internet, research free block list providers that can be configured within Exchange Server 2007. Next, configure your server NT2670Srv##B to use this provider using the Exchange Management Shell.

NOTES

NOTES

NOTES

NOTES

NOTES

NOTES

NOTES

NOTES

NOTES

NOTES

NOTES

NOTES

NOTES

NOTES

NOTES

NOTES

NOTES

NOTES